Spellbound
6

Published by
CJ FALLON
Ground Floor - Block B Liffey Valley Office Campus Dublin 22 Ireland

ISBN 978-0-7144-1640-3

First Edition March 2007
©
CJ Fallon

This Reprint September 2016

Printed by
W & G Baird Limited
Caulside Drive Antrim

Contents

Introduction

Spellbound, a series of seven books, encourages a multidimensional approach to spelling for children from Senior Infants to Sixth Class, while helping to develop phonological and phonemic awareness.

- Colour is used to highlight blends, digraphs, prefixes, onsets, rhymes, etc.
- Words are sorted into blocks of seven, chosen for their suitability and relevance in the modern Irish context.
- Each book has a wide range of activities, which reinforce the learning of each spelling.
- Four revision chapters throughout the book and three general revision chapters at the end help consolidate learned spellings.
- A section at the back of each book facilitates "end of week" tests. This allows ease of monitoring by both teachers and parents/guardians.
- In Fifth and Sixth Classes, the teacher may test the children on the twenty-five most appropriate words for his/her class each week.
- After the weekly test has been completed, the children may colour the grid on the last page of the book. This gives a visible record of his/her progress and affords an opportunity for integration with the Mathematics Curriculum.

| app | hu | inter | al |

Handwritten: Fun Friday

Block

1. apply ✓
   applaud ✗
   applause ✗
   apology ✗
   apologise ✗
   apostle ✗
   energy ✗

2. hunch ✓
   hungry ✗
   hunter ✗
   hundred ✗
   hurdle ✗
   hurry ✓
   hurried ✗

3. interest ✗
   interesting ✗
   international ✗
   intermediate ✗
   interview ✗
   interfere ✓
   intense ✗

4. insult ✗
   interrupt ✗
   disrupt ✗
   intend ✗
   extend ✗
   internal ✗
   external ✗

Bonus

1. _____
2. _____

Exercise 1 Dictionary Work

Write the **block** words that match these definitions.

(a) the feeling of hunger — *hungry*

(b) a means of saying sorry — *apology / apologise*

(c) power that provides heat or drives machines — *energy*

(d) a feeling you might be right — *hunch / intermediate*

(e) a number > 99 — *hundred*

(f) an obstacle to be cleared in a race — *hurdle*

Exercise 2 Unscramble the confused words in these sentences.

(a) My sister was unsure about which course to palpy for because many of them looked nespirtetig.
   (i) *apply* (ii) *interesting*

(b) The crowd of spectators riduhre to the stiles as the tntoliraiaenn match was about to kick off.
   (i) *hurried* (ii) *international*

(c) I don't mean to siltun you, but I wouldn't wear that tie to the job nreitveiw
   (i) *insult* (ii) *interview*

(d) The politician was advised not to nerirftere in the nlanetri affairs of the neighbouring country.
   (i) *interfere* (ii) *internal*

(e) The editor uriderh to print an qoplyga after the statements in the article were proven to be false.
   hurried *apology*

Exercise 3 Make as many words as you possibly can from the letters in the word INTERNATIONAL.

1. National	2. Inter	3. Natalie
4. Internal.	5. net	6. rat
7. Natan	8. rent.	9. era
10. ten	11. tan	12. tent
13. not	14. Tina	15. no.
16. on	17. in	18. Internet

Exercise 4 **Oops!** Looks like these **block** words have been chopped up.
Sort them out. Write the word.

inter   ult   (a) _interfere_

apo   gry   (b) _apostle._

en   ense   (c) _energy._

hun   end   (d) _hungry._

int   fere   (e) _intense._

dis   stle   (f) _disrupt._

ext   lause   (g) _extend._

ins   ergy   (h) _insult._

app   rupt   (i) _applause._

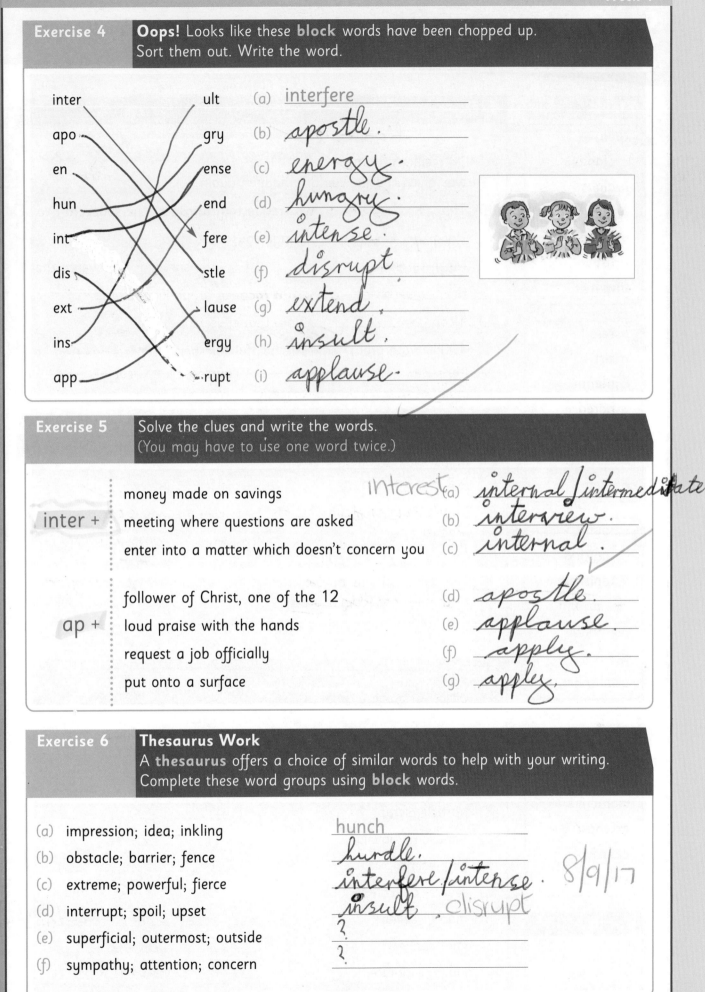

Exercise 5 Solve the clues and write the words.
(You may have to use one word twice.)

inter +

money made on savings   _interest_ (a) _internal / intermediate_

meeting where questions are asked   (b) _interview._

enter into a matter which doesn't concern you   (c) _internal._

ap +

follower of Christ, one of the 12   (d) _apostle._

loud praise with the hands   (e) _applause._

request a job officially   (f) _apply._

put onto a surface   (g) _apply._

Exercise 6 **Thesaurus Work**
A **thesaurus** offers a choice of similar words to help with your writing.
Complete these word groups using **block** words.

(a) impression; idea; inkling   _hunch_

(b) obstacle; barrier; fence   _hurdle._

(c) extreme; powerful; fierce   _interfere / intense._   _8/9/17_

(d) interrupt; spoil; upset   _insult, disrupt_

(e) superficial; outermost; outside   _?_

(f) sympathy; attention; concern   _?_

week 2

ar | ment | ass | ast | att | magic e

Block

5
- area ✗
- aroma ✓
- argue ✓
- argument ✗
- arguing ✗
- acute ✓
- dispute ✗

6
- assess ✗
- assist ✗
- assistant ✗
- assistance ✗
- assure ✗
- assurance ✗
- assume ✗

7
- astound ✗
- astonish ✗
- astonishment ✗
- astray ✗
- astronaut ✗
- atom ✗
- atmosphere ✗

8
- attic ✓
- attach ✗
- attract ✗
- attractive ✗
- attend ✓
- attack ✓
- attire ✓

Bonus
1. _____
2. _____

Exercise 1 — Complete these sentences using **block** words.

(a) The ~~dispute~~ argument was settled when an ~~astray~~ assurance. was given that it wouldn't happen again.

(b) The assistant ✗astronaut. was requested to inspect the spacecraft to dispute ✗ assess the damage caused at lift-off.

(c) Much to his assistance astonishment, the surveyor discovered that the attic. had never been properly insulated.

(d) 'I can assure. you, that these shoes are 100% waterproof.' said the helpful salesperson.

Exercise 2 — Write the **block** words that contain these smaller words.

(a) ran — assurance
(b) cut — acute.
(c) end — attend.
(d) sum — assume.
(e) put — dispute.
(f) gum — argument
(g) ton — astonish
(h) act — attractive
(i) ray — astray.
(j) men — astonishment.

Exercise 3 — Thesaurus work
Complete these word groups using **block** words.

(a) assault; charge; — attack
(b) clothing; dress; — attire
(c) off course; adrift; — astray ✗
(d) particle; scrap; — atom ✗
(e) handsome; lovely; — attractive
(f) be present; — attend.
(g) severe; critical; serious; — acute.
(h) mood; feeling; — atmosphere ✗ astonishm
(i) join; connect; — attach.
(j) judge; estimate; — assistant ✗

6

Exercise 4

List all the 5-letter words from **blocks 1** to **8** in column **A**.
Then sort them alphabetically in column **B**. If two words begin with the
same letter, look at the second letter. If the first two letters are the same,
look at the third letter. Example: ar**g**ue and ar**o**ma.
Argue comes first alphabetically.

a b c d e f g h i j k l m n o p q r s t u v w x y z

A list

1. apply
2. hunch
3. hurry.
4. aroma
5. argue
6. acute.
7. attic.

Alpha**B**etical list

1. acute
2. apply
3. argue
4. aroma
5. attic
6. hunch
7. hurry

Exercise 5

Circle every alternate (second) letter in the **wordsnake** to discover **8 block**
words. Write the words. There are 4 words in red and 4 words in black.

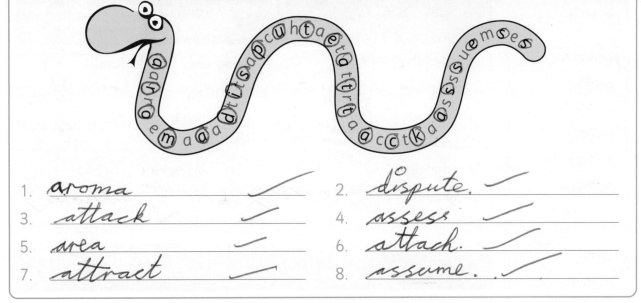

1. aroma
2. dispute.
3. attack
4. assess
5. area
6. attach.
7. attract
8. assume.

Exercise 6

Fill the wordboxes with letters that fit their shape.

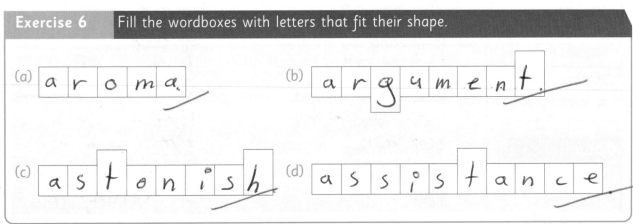

(a) a r o m a.

(b) a r g u m e n t.

(c) a s t o n i s h

(d) a s s i s t a n c e.

| ch | er | en | silent t | pol | pos | post |

Block

9 anchor
echo
choir
chorus
chemical
chemist
character

10 litter
glitter
listen
glisten
listener
fasten
bitter

11 police
policy
polite
polish
politics
politician
political

12 positive
position
postage
posture
postpone
possess
possession

Bonus

1. _____
2. _____

Exercise 1   Complete each sentence using **block** words.

(a) The soloist took the lead, and the rest of the ~~character~~ *choir* joined in during the ___ *choir* X *chorus* chorus.

(b) The ~~character~~ *chemist* was lucky to avoid injury when the *chemical* ~~postage~~ jar spilled over.

(c) 'Do you ever ___ *listen*, ?' asked his mother. 'I told you to ___ *position* those buttons.'

(d) There was a dull ___ *echo* as the ship's ~~position~~ *anchor* hit the seabed.

(e) It would be foolish to believe that all that ___ *glitters* *glistens* is made from gold.

Exercise 2   **Plurals**
Write the plural forms (more than one) of these **block** words. The plurals can be made by adding 's' – all except for one!

	singular	plural		singular	plural
(a)	chemist	*chemists*	(f)	choir	*choirs*
(b)	listener	*listeners*	(g)	anchor	*anchors*
(c)	politician	*pliticians*	(h)	position	*positions*
(d)	chemical	*chemicals*	(i)	possession	*possessions*
(e)	character	*characters*	(j)	echo	*echoes*

Exercise 3   **Thesaurus work**
Complete these word groups using **block** words.

(a) singers; vocalists;   *choir*

(b) sour-tasting; sharp;   *bitter*

(c) secure; tie-up;   *fasten*

(d) apothecary; pharmacist;   *chemist* / ~~chemist~~

(e) resound; repeat;   *echo*

(f) rubbish; refuse;   *litter*

(g) mannerly; courteous;   *positive* X *polite*

(h) make smooth; shine;   *glitter / glisten*

Exercise 4 Fill the word boxes with letters that fit their shape.
All begin with **p** and can be found between **blocks 11** and **12**.

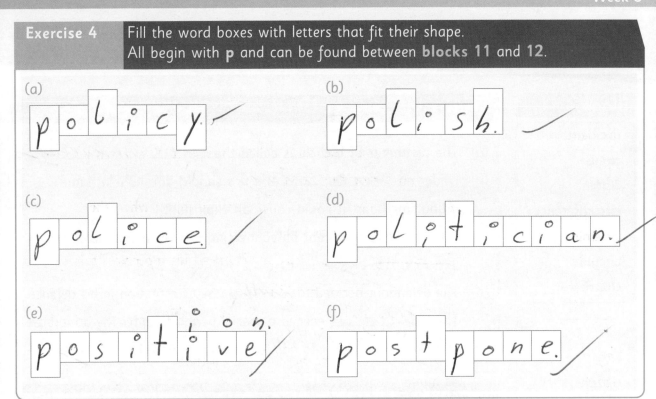

(a) p o l i c y

(b) p o l i s h

(c) p o l i c e

(d) p o l i t i c i a n

(e) p o s i t i v e / p o s i t i o n

(f) p o s t p o n e

Exercise 5 Complete these sentences using just 3 **block** words.

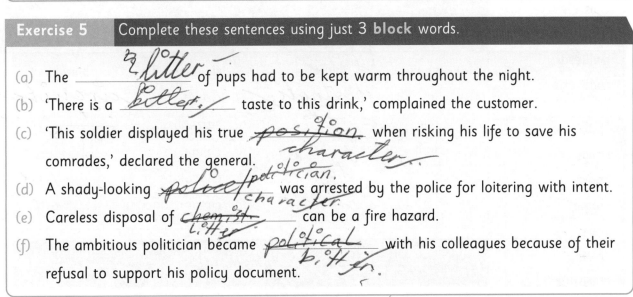

(a) The ___litter___ of pups had to be kept warm throughout the night.

(b) 'There is a ___bitter___ taste to this drink,' complained the customer.

(c) 'This soldier displayed his true ___position / character___ when risking his life to save his comrades,' declared the general.

(d) A shady-looking ___police / politician / character___ was arrested by the police for loitering with intent.

(e) Careless disposal of ___chemist / litter___ can be a fire hazard.

(f) The ambitious politician became ___political / bitter___ with his colleagues because of their refusal to support his policy document.

Exercise 6 **Crack the code!**
Find **block** words by solving these codes. Write the words.

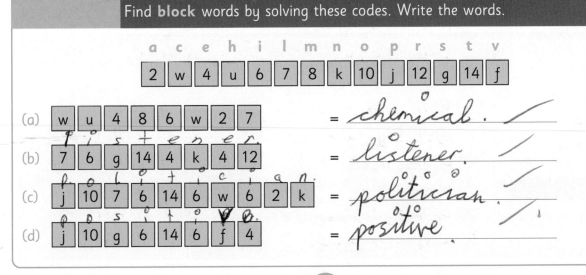

a	c	e	h	i	l	m	n	o	p	r	s	t	v
2	w	4	u	6	7	8	k	10	j	12	g	14	f

(a) w u 4 8 6 w 2 7 = ___chemical___

(b) 7 6 g 14 4 k 4 12 = ___listener___

(c) j 10 7 6 14 6 w 6 2 k = ___politician___

(d) j 10 g 6 14 6 f 4 = ___positive___

9

ci | i | ch | magic e

Block

13 accident
circus ✓
circle
circumference
circumstance
circular
circuit

14 cite
city
citizen
civil ✓
civilian
civilised
civilisation

15 chill
chilly
chant
chime ✓
chess ✓
chisel
chestnut

16 China
churn
chunk ✓
chose
choose
chariot
chocolate

Bonus

1. _____
2. _____

Exercise 1 — Complete each sentence using **block** words.

(a) The perimeter of a circle is called the *circumference*.

(b) Under no *circumstance*s should you light a flame if you smell gas. It could cause an explosion.

(c) We made the bulb light by connecting a wire to complete the ~~circus~~ *circuit* ✗ *cite*.

(d) The defendant decided to ~~cite~~ the Constitution in his defence.

(e) The *citizen* / *civilian* needed a special permit to enter the army base.

(f) She didn't mean for it to happen. It was a complete *accident*.

Exercise 2 — Plural

Write the plural form of these **block** words. The plurals can be made by adding 's' – all except for one.

	singular	plural		singular	plural
(a)	chestnut	chestnuts	(f)	circuit	circuits
(b)	circle	circles	(g)	citizen	citizens
(c)	chunk	chunks	(h)	chime	chimes
(d)	city	cities	(i)	chocolate	chocolates
(e)	chariot	chariots	(j)	circumstance	circumstances

Exercise 3 — List all the 5-letter words from **blocks 14** to **16** in column **A**. Then sort them alphabetically in column **B**.

a b c d e f g h i j k l m n o p q r s t u v w x y z

A list
1. civil
2. chill
3. chant
4. chime
5. chess
6. China
7. churn
8. chunk
9. chose

AlphaBetical list
1. chant
2. chess
3. chill
4. chime
5. China
6. chose
7. chunk
8. churn
9. civil

Exercise 4   Ring the twenty **block** words in the **wordsearch**.
The arrows show the directions of the words.

d	a	n	i	e	c	h	o	c	o	l	a	t	e	n
e	c	i	r	c	u	i	t	l	o	e	d	o	n	e
s	f	u	c	h	a	r	i	o	t	s	p	l	t	l
i	f	d	a	o	n	e	z	i	t	i	c	d	n	r
l	t	s	e	s	l	t	q	e	b	h	y	d	a	a
i	h	e	b	e	a	c	h	b	o	c	y	c	h	l
v	e	c	n	e	r	e	f	m	u	c	r	i	c	u
i	s	i	i	r	r	o	m	n	a	h	v	t	s	c
c	o	v	n	d	u	c	s	t	i	n	y	t	r
c	h	i	m	e	e	h	k	r	u	l	t	e	h	i
h	y	l	s	a	n	e	t	a	c	l	a	u	s	c
u	i	a	f	h	t	s	o	o	t	y	e	h	t	e
r	c	i	r	c	u	s	t	h	e	s	o	o	h	c
n	r	y	t	n	e	d	i	c	c	a	t	h	r	e
s	s	r	t	u	n	t	s	e	h	c	a	e	b	e

circus →
city ↓
chime →
chose ↓
accident ←
circuit →
civil ↓
chilly ↓
chariot →
chant ↑
circumference ←
citizen ←
chess ↓
churn ↓
chisel ↑
circular ↑
civilised ↑↓
chestnut ←
chocolate →
choose ←

Exercise 5   **See how clever you are!**
Fill in the things you now know.

(a) I know that the ringmaster introduces acts in a _circus_.

(b) I know that radius and diameter are parts of a _circle_.

(c) I know that the queen and pawn are pieces from the game of _chess_.

(d) I know that the country with the greatest population is _China_.

(e) I know that the Romans used _chariot_ s in great races.

(f) I know that a stone _chisel_ is part of a sculptor's equipment.

(g) I know that Berlin is the capital _city_ of Germany.

(h) I know that conkers are a game played using _chestnut_ s.

(i) I know that there are three 'e's in this word from **block 13**. _circumference_.

(j) I know that there are eight _chunk_ s in this bar of _chocolate_.

Oops! Yum! Make that seven! I've just eaten one of them.

| ex | sion | sive | tr | tion |

Block

17 extend
extension
examine
examination
expert
expertise
exhibition

18 expense
expensive
extent
extensive
experience
experiment
expel

19 express
expression
expose
expedition
extract
extreme
extremely

20 exhaust
exercise
extinct
exception
explanation
exploit
extraordinary

Bonus

1. _____
2. _____

Exercise 1
Complete each sentence using **block** words that end in **-ion**.

(a) The artist displayed her work at an _exhibition_.

(b) He gave her a bouquet of flowers as an _____ X X of his regret.

(c) The teacher required an _explanation_ for the pupil's absence.

(d) The builder was asked to supply an estimate for the _extention_ to the school.

(e) Doctor Burke gave the patient a thorough _exploit examination_ before recommending treatment.

(f) Tom Crean was a celebrated explorer who survived an _experience_ to the South Pole.

(g) It is said that the _expel_ proves the rule.

Exercise 2   Wordsnake
Write the twelve words that are in this **wordsnake**.

1. _examine_   2. _expertise_   3. _experience_
4. _expensive_   5. _experiment_   6. _extreme_
7. _exploit_   8. _extinct_   9. _exhaust_
10. _express_   11. _extract_   12. _exercise_

Exercise 3 — Crack the code!

Find **block** words by solving these codes. Write the words.

a	d	e	i	l	n	o	p	r	s	t	v	x	y
3	2	5	w	9	j	7	m	11	k	15	h	13	f

(a) `5 13 m 5 11 15` _expert._

(b) `5 13 m 5 9` _expel_

(c) `5 13 m 9 7 w 15` _exploit._

(d) `5 13 m 5 j k w h 5` _expensive._

(e) `5 13 15 11 3 7 11 2 w j 3 11 f` _extraordinary._

Exercise 4 — Thesaurus Work

Complete these word groups using **block** words.

(a) costly; dear; _expensive_

(b) check; inspect; _examine:_

(c) display; presentation; _exhibition._

(d) tire; wear out; _exhaust_

(e) games; activity; _exercise,_

(f) remove; throw out; _extract._

(g) notable; remarkable; _extraordinary_

(h) reveal; uncover; _expose._

(i) draw out; pull out; _exploit._

(j) quenched; died out; _expire_

Exercise 5

Write the **two** words that must be swapped in each sentence in order for the sentence to make sense.

(a) The pilot had to call on all his experience extensive in order to land the plane safely.

(i) _extensive_   (ii) _experience._

(b) You knew by his exhibition that the critic was most impressed by the quality of work in the expression.

(i) _expression_   (ii) _exhibition._

(c) The student came up with an unusual exercise for not completing his explanation.

(i) _explanation_   (ii) _exercise._

(d) Do not extremes this equipment to any expose of temperature.

(i) _expose_   (ii) _extremes._

| ary | en | pp | tion | magic e |

Block

21
ordinary
temporary
February
voluntary
necessary
January
library

22
instinct
instinctive
distinct
distinctive
entry
sentry
entrance

23
oppose
opposite
opposition
apply
application
appeal
approve

24
persuade
safely
safety
desperate
perforate
fortunate
separate

Bonus
1. _____
2. _____

Exercise 1 — Dictionary Work
Use **block** words to solve the following clues.
Write the words. All answers end in -**ary**.

(a) first month of the year — *January* ✓
(b) a collection of books — *library* ✓
(c) a short-term solution — *temporary* ✓
(d) do this for no pay — *voluntary* ✓
(e) mid-term break comes in this month — *February* ✓
(f) nothing special — *necessary* ✗ ordinary
(g) must have this one — *persuade* ✗ necessary

Exercise 2
Fill the wordboxes with letters which fit their shape.

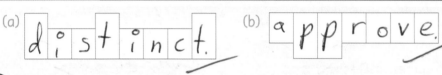

(a) d i s t i n c t ✓   (b) a p p r o v e ✓

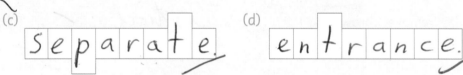

(c) s e p a r a t e ✓   (d) e n t r a n c e ✓

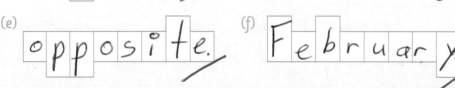

(e) o p p o s i t e ✓   (f) F e b r u a r y

Exercise 3 — Oops!
These words from **block 21** to **24** have been chopped up. Sort and write them.

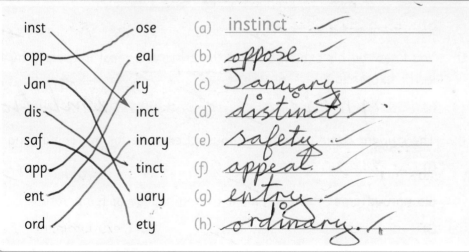

inst — ose
opp — eal
Jan — ry
dis — inct
saf — inary
app — tinct
ent — uary
ord — ety

(a) *instinct* ✓
(b) *oppose* ✓
(c) *January* ✓
(d) *distinct* ✓
(e) *safety* ✓
(f) *appeal* ✓
(g) *entry* ✓
(h) *ordinary* ✓

Exercise 4 Use every alternate letter in the **wordsnake** to discover the eight **block** words. There are four words in black and four words in red.

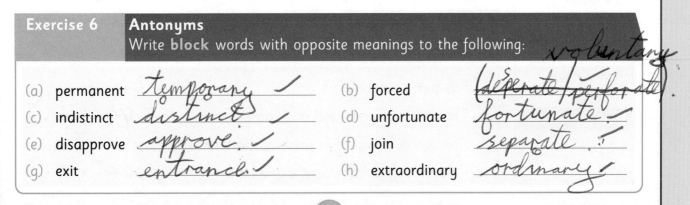

1. *application* ✓
2. *entrance*
3. *oppose* ✓
4. *temporary* ✓
5. *opposition* ✓
6. *ordinary* ✓
7. *separate* ✓
8. *distinct* ✓

13/10/17

Exercise 5 **Analogies**
Analogies compare things with a similar relationship.
Use **block** words to complete these analogies.

Example: **hoof** is to horse as **paw** is to dog

(a) Way-out is to exit as way-in is to… *entrance* (*entry*)

(b) June is to July as January is to… *February* ✓

(c) Picture is to gallery as book is to… *library* ✓

(d) Instinct is to instinctive as distinct is to… *distinctive* ✓

(e) Long-term is to permanent as short-term is to… *temporary* ✓

(f) Unlucky is to unfortunate as lucky is to… *fortunate* ✓

(g) Permit is to allow as consent is to… *persuade* *approve*

(h) Security-guard is to site as *sentry* is to barracks.

Exercise 6 **Antonyms**
Write **block** words with opposite meanings to the following:

voluntary

(a) permanent *temporary* ✓ (b) forced (*desperate / perforate*) ✓
(c) indistinct *distinct* ✓ (d) unfortunate *fortunate* ✓
(e) disapprove *approve* ✓ (f) join *separate* ✓
(g) exit *entrance* ✓ (h) extraordinary *ordinary* ✓

or | op | eq | magic e

Block

25
orbit
organ
organic
organise
organisation
ordeal
orchard

26
orphan
origin
original
originally
ornament
absorb
northern

27
evaporate
operate
operation
opinion
opening
operator
option

28
equal
equally
equate
equation
equator
equip
equipment

Bonus
1. _____
2. _____

Exercise 1   Thesaurus Work
Complete these word groups using **block** words.

(a) body part; keyboard;   *organ.*
(b) experience; suffering;   *ordeal.*
(c) cause; beginning;   *origin.*
(d) trinket; decoration;   *ornament.*
(e) circle; travel round;   *equator.*
(f) stray; parentless;   *orphan.*
(g) fruit field; apple yard;   _____
(h) baggage; supplies;   *equipment.*

Exercise 2   Unjumble the <u>confused</u> words in these sentences.

(a) You may have to pay more to buy <u>craingo</u> fruit and vegetables but in my <u>noinipo</u> it is worth it.
(i) *organic.*   (ii) *opinion.*

(b) The <u>oenginp</u> of the store was <u>lrinloiagy</u> planned for next month but had to be postponed.
(i) *opening.*   (ii) *originally.*

(c) The <u>rbtoi</u> of the satellite was planned so that it could study climate change in the <u>rrhntoen</u> hemisphere.
(i) *orbit.*   (ii) *northern.*

(d) The surgeon declared the <u>paioroetn</u> a complete success and the diseased <u>angro</u> was safely removed.
(i) *operation*   (ii) *organ.*

(e) The human rights <u>sraitonaogin</u> did its best to help end the <u>rodlea</u> of the aid worker who had been abducted.
(i) *organisation.*   (ii) *ordeal.*

Exercise 3   Dictionary Work
Write the **block** words that match these dictionary meanings.

(a) to turn to steam   *absorb.*
(b) imaginary line around mid-Earth   *equator.*
(c) person in charge of a piece of machinery *operator.*
(d) mathematical statement e.g. $2x = 8$ *equation.*

Exercise 4

List the 10 six-letter words from **blocks 23 to 28** in column **A**.
Then sort them alphabetically in column **B**.

a b c d e f g h i j k l m n o p q r s t u v w x y z

A list

1. oppose
2. appeal
3. safely
4. safety
5. ordeal
6. origin
7. absorb
8. option
9. equate
10. orphan

AlphaBetical list

1. appeal
2. absorb
3. appeal
4. oppose
5. option
6. ordeal
7. origin
8. orphan
9. safely
10. safety

equate
appeal
equate

Exercise 5

Search carefully through this **wordsearch** and find the twenty listed
block words. The arrows show the directions of the words.

e	a	n	o	r	t	h	e	r	n	t	i	b	r	o
e	e	o	p	e	t	n	i	g	i	r	o	k	n	o
q	q	r	t	s	n	o	i	n	i	p	o	w	l	e
u	u	t	i	b	e	y	o	n	c	e	p	h	o	s
e	a	h	o	f	a	r	e	y	l	a	e	d	r	o
a	t	o	n	e	r	s	v	e	v	e	r	y	p	o
l	o	r	i	g	i	n	a	l	l	y	a	s	h	t
o	r	c	h	a	r	d	p	l	a	u	t	u	a	n
c	h	h	e	b	u	l	o	d	g	a	e	r	n	e
i	s	a	n	s	n	e	r	b	r	e	t	s	i	m
n	o	n	e	o	r	n	a	m	e	n	t	t	o	p
a	c	c	o	r	n	i	t	o	q	u	i	c	h	i
g	o	e	o	b	u	q	e	q	u	a	l	l	y	u
r	e	q	u	a	t	i	o	n	a	t	n	a	u	q
o	q	u	a	l	i	n	t	y	l	p	i	u	q	e

orbit ←
origin ←
operate ↓
option ↓
originally →
organic ↑
orphan ↕
evaporate ↓
equation →
equator ↓
ordeal ←
absorb ↓
opinion ←
equip ←
northern →
orchard →
ornament →
equal ↓
equally →
equipment ↑

17

Revision – Weeks 1 to 8

Exercise 1   Complete the sentences by adding words that end in **-ion**.

(a) If one party is in government then the other parties are in _composition._ ✗

(b) You must make an _application_ for a license in order to get one.

(c) The condemned prisoner was given the _option_ of execution by hanging or firing-squad.

(d) The event went off most successfully and the organisers were praised for their excellent _organisation_.

(e) Careful checks were made on the equipment before the explorer set off on his _expedition_ into the jungle.

(f) A team of forensic scientists conducted a thorough _examination_ of the crime scene.

(g) Many believe that the Egyptians had the most advanced _civilization_ of ancient times.

(h) Help was requested by the student as the mathematical _equation_ ✗ proved too difficult to solve.

Exercise 2   There is one spelling mistake in each sentence. Find the mistake and write the word correctly.

(a) The prize was divided equelly among the three winners. — _equally_

(b) Our local libeerary was closed for three months for extensive redecoration. — _library_

(c) 'We were extreemly lucky to get a draw in that match,' admitted the visiting manager. — _extremely_

(d) The carpenter was fortunate not to lose his finger when he had an accident with the chisle. — _chisel_

(e) Emergency services rushed to the scene of the incident at the chemicle factory. — _chemical_

(f) The dispute between the two boys was settled when neither could remember what caused the arguement. — _argument_

(g) 'I didn't mean to insult you. Please accept my apolagy.' — _apology_

(h) 'In my opinion, organic vegetables have to be a healthier optsion for consumers,' said the minister. — _option_

Exercise 3 — Analogies
Use **block** words to complete these analogies.

Example: dentist is to mouth as optician is to eye.

(a) Loft is to barn as _attic_ is to house.

(b) Pilot is to plane as _astronaut_ is to spaceship.

(c) Drink is to thirsty as eat is to _hungry_.

(d) Unit is to ten as _hundred_ is to thousand.

(e) Inside is to outside as internal is to _external arrival_ ~~external~~

(f) Spaghetti is to Italy as rice is to _China_.

(g) Fragrance is to flower as _scent aroma_ is to coffee.

(h) Cube is to sphere as square is to _circle_.

(i) Rectangle is to rectangular as circle is to _circular_.

(j) Cosmonaut is to Russia as _Canada_ is to America.

(k) Eye is to look as ear is to _hear_.

(l) Cheap is to inexpensive as dear is to _expensive_.

(m) South is to southern as north is to _Northern_.

Exercise 4
Examine is an example of the thirteen words that can be found from blocks **1** to **22** that begin and end with the same letter.
List the words in column **A**. Then sort them alphabetically in column **B**.

a b c d e f g h i j k l m n o p q r s t u v w x y z

A list

1. area ✓
2. aroma ✓
3. examine ✓
4. expertise ✓
5. expense
6. expensive
7. extensive
8. experience
9. expose
10. extreme ✓
11. exercise
12. entrance ✓
13. example
   hunch

Alpha**B**etical list

1. area
2. aroma
3. entrance
4. examine
5. exercise
6. extreme
7. extensive
8. experience
9. _____
10. _____
11. expertise
12. examine
13. hunch

er | ly | li | ight | pro | magic e

Block

29 gender
male
female
masculine
feminine
father
mother

30 likely
lively
livestock
linen
lining
lightly
lily

31 fright
frighten
flight
lighthouse
height
eight
weight

32 episode
compose
propose
proposal
disclose
hopeless
hopeful

Bonus
1. _____
2. _____

Exercise 1 — Crack the code!
Use **block** words to solve the clues. Write them.

(a) a stallion is a _female_ horse
(b) a mare is a _male_ horse
(c) your dad is your _father._
(d) your mum is your _mother._
(e) a flower associated with Easter _lily_
(f) animals kept on a farm _livestock._
(g) associated with being manly _masculine._
(h) a loud bang could give you this _fright._

Exercise 2
The word **LIGHTLY** has the It Goes Home Tonight pattern. Use **block 31** to complete the following. Add seven of your own.

(a) height
(b) eight
(c) fright
(d) frighten
(e) weight
(f) flight
(g) lighthouse

(h) bright.
(i) light
(j) lightly
(k) brighten.
(l) lighten.
(m) brightly.
(n) frightful.

Exercise 3
These **block** words have been chopped up. Sort and write them.

fr · gen · lin · fe · com · hope · dis · hope
en · ful · ight · less · close · pose · der · male

(a) frighten.
(b) gender
(c) linen.
(d) female.
(e) compose
(f) HOPEFUL.
(g) disclose.
(h) hopeless

Exercise 4 Unscramble the confused words in these sentences. Write them.

(a) It is the melefa of the lion family that is more aggressive.   *female*

(b) Haggis is a Scottish delicacy made with the inglni
of a sheep's stomach.   *lining*

(c) I was late home from school and missed the final sopieed
of my favourite TV show.   *episode*

(d) The journalist was threatened with imprisonment for
refusing to lsocside the source of his story.   *dispose*

(e) You fill in the renged portion of the application form by ticking
either the lame or leefam box.
   (i) *gender*   (ii) *male*   (iii) *female*

(f) There was a posporla before the council to close the old manned githsohuel
and they were lufophe that a new automatic one would replace it.
   (i) *proposal*   (ii) *lighthouse*   (iii) *hopeful*

Exercise 5 Locate the words that contain these smaller words.

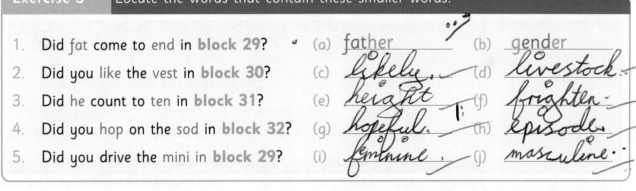

1. Did fat come to end in **block 29**?   (a) *father*   (b) *gender*
2. Did you like the vest in **block 30**?   (c) *likely*   (d) *livestock*
3. Did he count to ten in **block 31**?   (e) *height*   (f) *frighten*
4. Did you hop on the sod in **block 32**? (g) *hopeful*   (h) *episode*
5. Did you drive the mini in **block 29**? (i) *feminine*   (j) *masculine*

Exercise 6 Start from the centre of the spiral and work outwards to reveal the
12 words from **blocks 29** to **32**. Write the words.

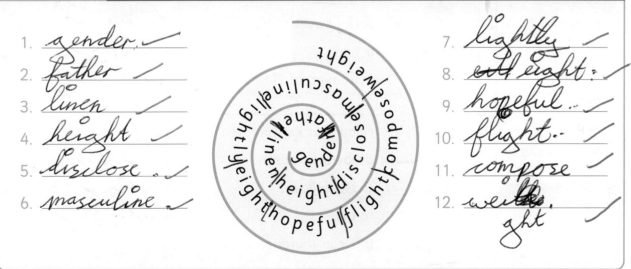

1. *gender*
2. *father*
3. *linen*
4. *height*
5. *disclose*
6. *masculine*

7. *lightly*
8. *eight*
9. *hopeful*
10. *flight*
11. *compose*
12. *weight*

| pur | sy | sym | y | py | ff | cc |

Block

33 purchase
purpose
purple
purely
purify – clean.
pursue – follow
pursuit – after something

34 syllable
syrup
symbol
symptom
sympathy
sympathise
sympathetic

35 pygmy – dwarf
pyramid
pyjamas
offend
offence
offensive
traffic

36 occasion
occasionally
occupy
occupation
occur
success
accommodation

Bonus

1. _____
2. _____

Exercise 1 Write the **block** words associated with the following.

(a) buy — *purchase*
(b) filter — *purify*
(c) Egypt — *piradmid*
(d) follow — *pursue*
(e) pancakes — *syrup*
(f) crime — *offence*
(g) motorway — *traffic*
(h) victory — *success*

Exercise 2 Complete these sentences using **block** words.

(a) The *purpose* of their visit was to *purchase* property overseas which they might *occasion*ally rent to friends.

(b) The chemical *symbol* for gold is AU.

(c) It is a criminal *offence* to use a mobile phone in moving *traffic*.

(d) On the *occasion* of their golden anniversary the couple was given a present of a meal for two plus *accommandation* at a luxurious hotel.

(e) 'Did it not *occur* to you that the bleeding was a *symptom* of a more serious complaint?' said the doctor.

Exercise 3 Write the correct words from **blocks 33 to 36**.

sy+
(a) feeling sorry for somebody — *sympathy*
(b) part of a word — *syllable*
(c) sticky sweet sauce — *syrup*
(d) a sign — *symbol*
(e) a warning of illness — *symptom*

(f) colour, darker than red — *purple*
(g) deliberate, reason — *purpose*

pur+
(h) chase, follow — *pursue*
(i) to buy — *purchase*
(j) to clean thoroughly — *purify*

Exercise 4 Thesaurus Work
Complete these word groups using **block** words.

(a) job; employment; *occupation.*

(b) clean; disinfect; *purify.*

(c) dwarf; midget; *purpose. pygmy*

(d) point; use; *sympathy. purpose*

(e) pity; understanding; *sympathy.*

(f) moment; opportunity; *occasion.*

(g) buy; acquire; *purchase.*

(h) feature; sign; warning; *symbol.*

Exercise 5
Locate the twenty words from **blocks 33** to **36** in this **wordsearch**.
Enter them in the spaces provided below as you find them.
The words go either across ➝ or down ↓ .

Write the words.

1. symbol
2. *occur.*
3. *syrup*
4. *offensive.*
5. *purely.*
6. *purchase*
7. *symptom.*
8. *accommodation.*
9. *pygmy.*
10. *occupy.*
11. *purpose.*
12. *pursue.*
13. *pyramid*
14. *traffic.*
15. *sympathy.*
16. *occupation.*
17. *pursuit.*
18. *syllable.*
19. *success.*
20. *offence.*

s	y	r	s	y	m	b	o	l	o	o	c	c	u	r
y	r	y	u	y	r	u	p	u	r	p	o	s	e	t
r	u	a	c	c	o	m	m	o	d	a	t	i	o	n
a	p	o	c	o	s	o	p	y	g	m	y	m	y	p
p	u	r	e	l	y	y	l	e	r	u	s	y	p	o
s	r	p	s	y	m	p	t	o	m	s	y	o	o	c
s	c	u	s	q	p	u	r	s	u	e	r	c	f	c
y	h	p	y	r	a	m	i	d	o	e	o	c	f	u
l	a	r	c	c	t	r	a	f	f	i	c	q	e	p
l	s	s	o	m	h	m	o	d	f	c	c	f	n	a
a	e	u	e	s	y	a	t	i	e	c	u	f	m	t
b	y	s	y	y	m	b	o	l	n	u	p	i	i	i
l	p	p	u	r	s	u	i	t	c	s	y	c	d	o
e	p	u	r	u	m	y	s	r	e	u	c	c	o	n
p	a	x	h	p	o	f	f	e	n	s	i	v	e	x

17/11/17

out | rr | ob | le | double letters | magic e

Block

37
outer
outburst
outrage
outlook
outfit
outcome
outskirts

38
terrible
terrier
terrific
terrify
territory
terrace
terrorise

39
obey
object
objection
obtain
oblige
obvious
obstacle

40
tennis
annoy
difficult
rubbish
tunnel
opponent
scribble

Bonus

1. _____
2. _____

Exercise 1   **O U** do know the answers to all of these.
Write the **block** words containing the **OU** sound.

(a) The lady bought a new _outfit_ for the wedding.

(b) A new bus depot was to be built on the _outskirts_ of the city.

(c) The opposite of inner is _outer_.   outburst

(d) The politician responded with an angry _outrage_ in the Dáil.

(e) A strike may be averted depending on the _outburst_ of the peace talks.   outcome

(f) 'Despite the rain all week, the _outcome_ for the weekend is better,' announced the weather forecaster.   outlook

(g) The Holocaust was an _outrage_ against the Jewish people.

Exercise 2   Underline the word that cannot be made from all or some of the letters in the first word. Write the word.

(a) outburst: stub, sour, stout, <u>roast</u>, trout   _roast_

(b) terrace: tear, trace, create, <u>actor</u>, react   _actor_

(c) outrage: true, route, great, grout, <u>trade</u>   _trade_

(d) scribble: rise, bile, <u>cable</u>, scribe, bible   _cable_

(e) obstacle: stale, least, <u>tackle</u>, closet, boast   _tackle_

(f) terrific: cert, <u>fort</u>, tier, rice, fire   _fort_

(g) terrible: <u>rear</u>, rile, leer, belt, tribe   _rear_

Exercise 3   **Dictionary Work**
Write the **block** words that match these definitions.

(a) on the fringes   _outskirts_

(b) what will happen   _outcome_

out +   (c) a view to the future   _outlook_

(d) intense anger   _out burst/rage_

(e) clothes / garments   _outfit_

24

Exercise 4 | Use **block** words to solve the following clues. Write the words. They all contain a double letter.

(a) I can never understand why you must sit in the stand and stand on the
terrace !

(b) In the USA they call this trash, but we call it _rubbish_.

(c) Wimbledon is the home of the premier tournament in the game of _territory_. *tennis*

(d) If you thought that clue (a) was easy then this one must be _difficult_.

(e) A Highland _terrier_ is small, black and white dog.

(f) An underground passageway is called a _tunnel_ .

(g) This person plays against you. _opponent_.

(h) To make somebody slightly angry. _annoy_

(i) To write carelessly. _scribble_ .

Exercise 5 | The word **terr / if / ic** can be broken into three syllables. Sort the following words into groups of two-syllable and three-syllable words.

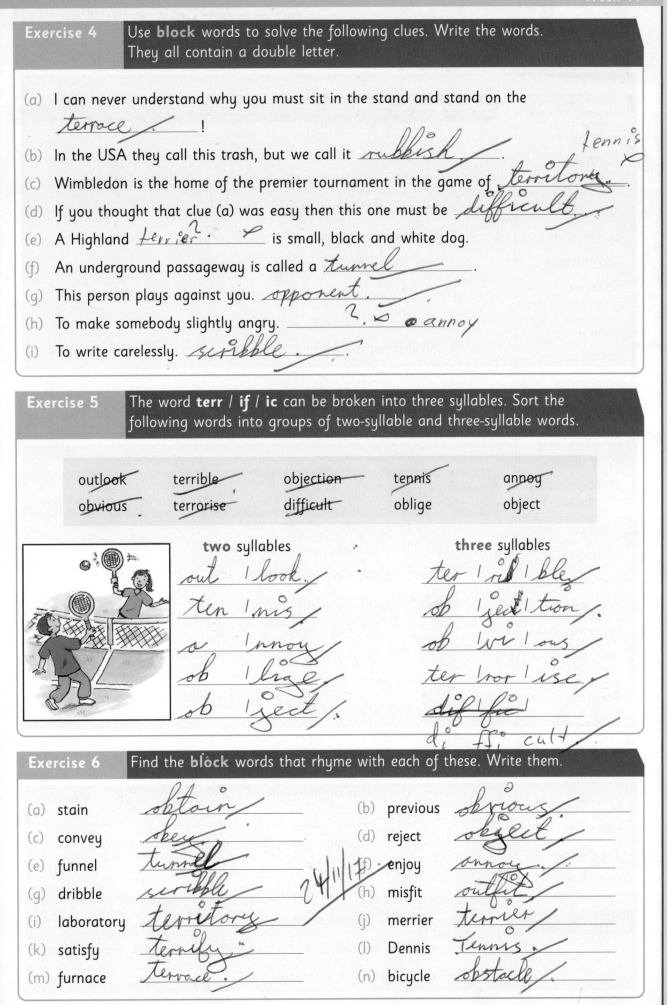

| outlook | terrible | objection | tennis | annoy |
| obvious | terrorise | difficult | oblige | object |

two syllables
out / look
ten / nis
a / nnoy
ob / lige
ob / ject

three syllables
ter / ri / ble
ob / jec / tion
ob / vi / ous
ter / ror / ise
~~dif / fic~~
di / ffi / cult

Exercise 6 | Find the **block** words that rhyme with each of these. Write them.

(a) stain _obtain_

(b) previous _obvious_

(c) convey _obey_

(d) reject _object_

(e) funnel _tunnel_

24/11/17

(f) enjoy _annoy_

(g) dribble _scribble_

(h) misfit _outfit_

(i) laboratory _territory_

(j) merrier _terrier_

(k) satisfy _terrify_

(l) Dennis _tennis_

(m) furnace _terrace_

(n) bicycle _obstacle_

Block

41
command
commandment
commence
comment
commentary
commentator
common

42
commute
commuter
communal
committee
communion
community
communicate

43
compact
compare
comparison
company
companion— friend it you sub someone.
compensate—
compatible -

44
competitor
competition
compete
complete
complain
complaint
compliment

Bonus

1. _____
2. _____

Exercise 1   Complete these sentences using **block** words.

(a) The performance will *commence* at 8 pm sharp.

(b) There is a variety of activities available to all people in the *committee* centre.

(c) The document wouldn't print because the computer wasn't *compatible* with the printer.

(d) The chef was pleased to receive the *compliment* (comment or) for the quality of the meal.

(e) If you are not happy with the service, don't be afraid to *complain*.

(f) Many people live a long way from their place of work and must *commute* each day.

Exercise 2   **I'm still learning.**
Look at all the things I know now.

(a) I know that a soldier must obey the *command* of an officer.

(b) I know that we elect a *committee* to run a club or organisation.

(c) I know that there is no known cure for the *comment* cold.

(d) I know that in Roman times people used to wash in *communal* baths.

(e) I know that CD stands for *compact* disc.

(f) I know that bus lanes are a help for people who *commute* to work.

(g) I know that most airlines will *compensate* you if your luggage gets lost.

(h) I know that to compare one item with another is to make a *comparison*.

(i) I know that a *commentator* gives the commentary on a football match.

(j) I know that if I get all of these completed correctly you will pay me a *compliment*.

26

Exercise 3 — Crack the code!
Solve the codes and write the words. They are not all **block** words.

The codes `J 4 S S 2 F Y` and `J 4 S Q 1 G 2` stand for the words
c o m m e n t and c o m p a r e.

(a) `J 4 S Q 1 J Y` compact

(b) `S 4 S 2 F Y` moment

(c) `J 4 S 2 Y` comet

(d) `G 2 Q 2 1 Y` repeat

(e) `J 4 S S 2 F J 2` commence

(f) `J 4 G Q 4 G 1 Y 2` corporate

I did not need the help of a `Q 1 G 2 F Y` parent .

Exercise 4 — Alphabetical Order
List all the the words ending in **e** from **blocks 41** to **44** in column **A**.
Then sort them alphabetically in column **B**.

A list

1. commence
2. commute
3. committee
4. communicate
5. compare
6. compensate
7. compatible
8. compete
9. complete

Alpha**B**etical list

1. commence
2. committee
3. communicate
4. commute
5. compare
6. compatible
7. compensate
8. compete
9. complete

Exercise 5
Write the plural form of these words by simply adding **s**.
There are two exceptions.

(a) comment: comments

(b) complaint: complaints

(c) commuter: commuters

(d) competition: competitions

(e) committee: committees

(f) community: communities

(g) company: companys

(h) competitor: competitors

27

con | or | y | re | silent w

Block

45 concern
concerned
concentrate
conceal
conference
conclude
concert

46 absorb
evaporate
elevator
sponsor
factory
observatory
laboratory

47 recover
recovery
recommend
recognise
refuse
refusal
reflection

48 answer
sword
written
wreck
science
scientist
scissors

Bonus

1. _____
2. _____

Exercise 1 Thesaurus Work
Complete these word groups using **block** words.

(a) hide; obscure; cover; *conceal*
(b) end; finish; complete; *conclude*
(c) supporter; backer; *sponsor*
(d) worry; anxiety; *concern*
(e) dry up; disappear; *evaporate*
(f) know; identify; *recognize*
(g) draw in; soak up; *absorb*
(h) reject; decline; *refuse.*
(i) regain; repossess; *recover*
(j) suggest; put forward; *recommend*

Exercise 2
Use every alternate letter to discover the eight **block** words in the **wordsnake**. Write the words. There are 4 words in red and 4 words in black.

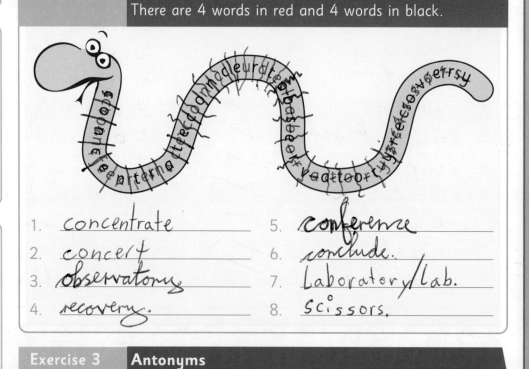

1. *concentrate*
2. *concert*
3. *observatory*
4. *recovery.*
5. *conference*
6. *conclude.*
7. *Laboratory/lab.*
8. *scissors.*

Exercise 3 Antonyms
Write **block** words with opposite meanings to these.

(a) reveal *conceal*   (b) oral *written*
(c) commence *conclude*   (d) accept *refuse*
(e) deteriorate *recover*   (f) question *answer*

Exercise 4 Suffixes

All the following words have had the suffix **ing** added to them.
Write the original form of the word in the spaces provided.

(a) concerning *concern*

(b) refusing *refuse*

(c) concentrating *concentrate.*

(d) evaporating *evaporate*

(e) concealing *conceal*

(f) sponsoring *sponsor*

(g) concluding *conclude.*

(h) recommending *recommend*

(i) absorbing *absorb.*

(j) recognising *recognise*

(k) answering *answer.*

(l) wrecking *wreck.*

Exercise 5 Complete each sentence using **block** words.

(a) The Aid agency said it was very *concerned* by the developments and was now going to *concentrate* its efforts on providing shelter for the homeless.

(b) After many long hours of research in her *laboratory* the eminent *scientist* was able to *conclude* that the experiment was a complete success.

(c) It has been *written* by many authors that the pen is mightier than the *sword*.

(d) 'Because of your *refusal* to *recognise* the court,' said the judge, 'I'm going to *recommend* that you spend three months as a guest of the state in order to help you *recover* from your memory loss!'

(e) 'Take the *elevator* to the fifth floor where you can enter the *observatory*. for a marvellous view of the night sky,' said the scientist.

Exercise 6 The following words have been written with their silent letters missing. Write the words correctly.

Example: **nome** + **g** = *gnome*

(a) sience + c = *science*

(b) reck + w = *wreck*

(c) sord + w = *sword*

(d) sissors + c = *sissos*

(e) ritten + w = *written*

(f) sientist + c = *scientist.*

Block

49
- mammal
- musical
- material
- festival
- carnival
- sandal
- vandal —graphetee on walls.

50
- valve
- vandalism
- signal
- punctual
- principal
- annual
- annually

51
- remove
- removal
- usual
- usually
- nature
- natural
- naturally

52
- climb
- dumb
- tomb
- gnome
- rhyme
- rhythm
- rhubarb —fruit.

Bonus

1. _____
2. _____

Exercise 1 — Dictionary Work

Solve these clues to make **block** words that end in **al**

(a) cloth used to make clothes — ~~sandal~~ material
(b) open-toed shoe worn in summer — sandala
(c) drama told through music — musical
(d) a sign given to another — signal
(e) this happens once a year — annually
(f) a destructive person — vandal
(g) no artificial ingredients — natural
(h) got here just in time — punctual
(i) another name for a feast/carnival — festival

Exercise 2 — Be careful!

Unjumble these **block** words. Write them.

(a) mmmlaa — mammal
(b) dalsan — sandal
(c) ciumsal — musical
(d) emogn — gnome
(e) aubrhrb — rhubarb
(f) bomt — tomb
(g) tanreu — nature
(h) bimcl — climb
(i) nnulaa — annual
(j) emrvoe — remove

Exercise 3

Fill in the boxes with letters that fit their shape.

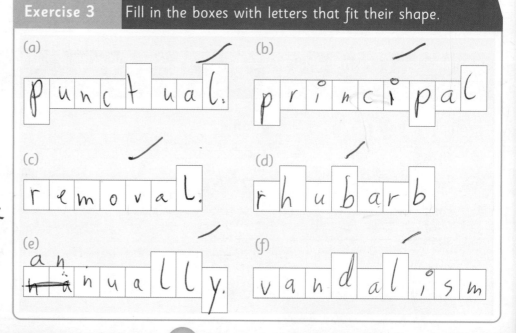

(a) p u n c t u a l.
(b) p r i n c i p a l
(c) r e m o v a l.
(d) r h u b a r b
(e) a n n u a l l y.
(f) v a n d a l i s m

Exercise 4

Start from the centre of the spiral and work outwards to reveal 12 **block** words. Write the words in the spaces provided.

1. usually
2. natural
3. rythem
4. carnival
5. dumb
6. principle

7. removal
8. nature
9. vandalism
10. tomb
11. mammal
12. value

Exercise 5

Locate the twenty words from **blocks 49** to **52** in this **wordsearch**.
Enter them in the spaces provided below as you find them.
The words go either across ➝ or down ↓.

Write the words.

1. principal
2. musical
3. rhubarb
4. mammal
5. usually
6. natural
7. tomb
8. signal
9. rhyme
10. rhythm
11. removal
12. carnival
13. punctual
14. annually
15. annual
16. vandal
17. remove
18. valve
19. climb
20. _____

r	h	y	m	u	s	i	c	a	l	q	a	r	b	p
h	n	a	t	u	r	v	a	n	d	a	n	l	t	r
y	v	b	r	h	u	b	a	r	b	v	n	o	m	i
t	a	m	a	m	m	a	l	t	o	a	u	m	b	n
h	l	i	q	l	a	r	h	n	b	n	a	r	r	c
y	v	e	m	o	t	e	m	a	t	d	l	e	h	i
r	e	m	o	v	e	v	u	s	u	a	l	l	y	p
e	r	e	c	a	r	n	i	v	a	l	y	r	t	a
m	m	b	t	o	i	m	b	n	a	c	t	u	h	l
o	c	l	i	n	a	t	u	r	a	l	v	e	m	l
v	l	y	r	a	l	e	m	o	s	i	g	n	a	l
a	u	a	l	t	l	y	c	a	r	m	n	i	v	q
l	m	n	s	u	i	c	t	o	m	b	a	l	u	s
c	l	i	m	r	h	y	m	e	a	n	n	u	a	l
s	i	g	n	e	a	l	p	u	n	c	t	u	a	l

15/12/17

ery ur silent n, g, b

Block

53
- machine
- machinery
- jewel
- jeweller
- jewellery
- monastery
- surgery

54
- surgeon
- urban
- urgent
- urgency
- further
- burglar
- survey

55
- suburban
- suburb
- turf
- turkey
- turnip
- adverb
- superb

56
- column
- condemn
- solemn – promise
- foreign
- design
- limb
- crumb

Bonus

1. _____
2. _____

Exercise 1

There are 11 words to be formed with **ur** as a central syllable. Write them.
- Only one is not to be found in **blocks 53** to **55**.

s
f
b + **ur** +
t
sub

ther
gery
vey
ban
key
f
nip
glar
b
geon

1. surgery
2. further
3. burglar
4. turnip
5. turkey
6. turf
7. suburban
8. suburb
9. surgeon
10. survey
11. ~~urgent~~
urban

Exercise 2

Accept the challenge!
Make at least 21 four-letter and 12 five-letter words using the letters in the word **MONASTERY**.
Each letter can only be used once in each word.

four-letter words

1. Mona
2. star
3. nose
4. nest
5. tear
6. stay
7. hame
8. omen
9. ones
10. stem
11. some
12. toes
13. tyte
14. yarn
15. Troy
16. ores
17. meat
18. oars
19. rats
20. soar
21. rose

five-letter words

1. omens
2. rents
3. roast
4. roman
5. neats
6. Snore
7. yarns
8. storm
9. senor
10. Trogs
11. trams
12. snare

Exercise 3 — Synonyms

Write the associated **block** word for each of these words.

(a) city ~~monastery~~ *suburban* urban
(b) coal turf
(c) thief burglar
(d) arm limb
(e) grammar adverb
(f) Christmas turkey
(g) doctor surgeon
(h) monk monastery
(i) morsel crumb
(j) vegetable turnip

Exercise 4

Complete these sentences using **block** words.

(a) In days past it was gathered by hand, but today we have _further_ machinery to assist in the production of t _urkey / turnip_

(b) Having studied the x-rays the _surgeon_ stressed the ~~suburb~~ surgeon of the operation if the affected _limb_ was to be saved.

(c) The renowned _survey_ was presented with the priceless _burglar_ and asked to _condemn_ a piece of _jewellery_ to be presented to the visiting _monastery_ head of state.

Exercise 5

There is one spelling mistake in each sentence.
Ring the word. Write the word.

(a) The survey revealed that most people were in favour of a name change for the (supurban) estate. suburban

(b) The teacher gave the instruction to write two (columbs), one containing all the adjectives, the other all the adverbs. columns

(c) The restaurant offered a choice of either parsnip or (tornip) to accompany the turkey meal. turnip

(d) If a jeweller sells jewellery then who sells (machinary?) machinery

(e) 'I must admit,' said the judge, 'that I have not been offered one crumb of evidence with which to (conthem) the accused.' condemn

(f) The (souperb) skill of the foreign players was praised by the coach. superb

(g) The eminent (sturgeon) carried out the delicate operation with great skill. surgeon

(h) When the old (monastary) was excavated, magnificent pieces of jewellery were discovered. monastery

Exercise 1	**Alphabetical Order**

There are 17 words that end in -**y** to be found between **blocks 29** and **44**.
List the words in column **A**. Then sort them alphabetically in column **B**.

A list

1. _____
2. _____
3. _____
4. _____
5. _____
6. _____
7. _____
8. _____
9. _____
10. _____
11. _____
12. _____
13. _____
14. _____
15. _____
16. _____
17. _____

Alpha**B**etical list

1. _ _ _ _ _
2. _ _ _ _ _ _ _ _ _ _
3. _ _ _ _ u _ _ _ _
4. _ _ _ _ _ _
5. _ _ _ _ _ _
6. _ k _ _ _ _
7. _ _ _ _ _ _
8. _ _ _ _ _ _
9. _ _ _ _ _ _
10. _ c _ _ _ _ _ _ _ _ _
11. _ _ _ _ _ _
12. _ _ _ _ l _
13. _ _ _ _ _ _
14. _ _ _ _ _ _
15. _ _ _ _ _ _
16. _ _ _ _ _ _ _
17. _ _ _ _ _ _ _ _

Exercise 2	**Analogies**

Use **block** words to complete these analogies.

Example: toe is to foot as finger is to hand.

(a) Country is to rural as town is to _____.

(b) Usual is to usually as natural is to *naturally*.

(c) Disclose is to reveal as hide is to *conceal*.

(d) Club is to golf as racquet is to *tennis*.

(e) Mother is to feminine as father is to *masculine*.

(f) Helpful is to helpless as hopeful is to *hopeless*.

(g) Machine is to machinery as jewel is to *jewellery*.

(h) Noun is to adjective as verb is to *adverb*.

(i) Legal is to legalise as sympathy is to *sympathise*.

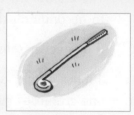

Exercise 3	Write the correct **block** word under each picture.

(a)

(b)

(c)

(d)

_____

(e)

(f)

(g)

(h)

_____

Exercise 4	Locate these items lost between **blocks 33** and **52**.

(a) a set of night clothes: (Wk 10)   _pyjamas._

(b) a toeless shoe: (Wk 14)   _____

(c) a sunken ship: (Wk 13)   _____

(d) a series of houses joined together: (Wk 11)   _____

(e) golden, sticky substance used in cooking: (Wk 10)   _____

(f) colour made by mixing red and blue: (Wk 10)   _____

(g) needed for causing a jam on the roads: (Wk 10)   _____

(h) two-sided, cutting implement: (Wk 13)   _____

(i) filling for a tart, other than apple: (Wk 14)   _____

(j) needed to fill the bins: (Wk 11)   _____

(k) another word for yearly: (Wk 14)   _____

Exercise 5	**Antonym**
	Find words with opposite meanings to these between **blocks 29** and **44**.

(a) heavily (Wk 9)   _____

(b) feminine (Wk 9)   _____

(c) failure (Wk 10)   _____

(d) disobey (Wk 11)   _____

(e) inner (Wk 11)   _____

(f) hopeless (Wk 9)   _____

(g) insult (Wk 12)   _____

(h) easy (Wk 11)   _____

(i) incomplete (Wk 12)   _____

(j) rare (Wk 12)   _____

35

| ty | y | or | sion | mi |

Block

57 type
typewriter
typist
typhoon – *violent tropical storm*
typical
nylon – *synthetic material used for clothing*
hygiene – *cleanliness*

58 major – *greater in number or quality*
majority – *greater over-half number*
minor – *lesser*
minority – *smaller party voting together*
junior
senior
seniority – *the fact or state of being older or in a higher value of rank*

59 military
minister – *head of the government*
ministry – *government department*
minuscule – *very small voting together*
minute
minus
mischief – *annoying but not malicious behaviour*

60 radon – *radioactive gaseous element*
divide
division
revise
revision
cylinder
physical – *of the body*

Bonus

1. _____
2. _____

Exercise 1

Use **block** words to solve the clues. Write them. (One word is used twice.)

(a) man-made material — ~~typical~~ . nylon

(b) senior army rank — military

(c) violent tropical storm — typhoon

(d) sixty seconds — minutes

(e) 28 ÷ 7 = 4 — division

(f) state of cleanliness — hygiene

(g) more than half — majority

(h) person who types — typist   of minisul

(i) very small piece, other than minute — ~~majorious~~ .very sma

(j) senior person in government — seniority   minister

Exercise 2

Put these words into groups of two and three syllables. There are 2 for each group. e.g. **di / vi / sion** has 3 syllables.

	two syllables	**three** syllables
(a) nylon	ny / lon	ty / pi / cil
(b) typical	ra / don	phy / si / cal
(c) physical		
(d) radon	ray-don ~~rat-don~~	

Exercise 3

Crack the code!
Find **block** words by solving these codes. Write the words.

a	c	d	e	f	h	i	l	m	n	o	p	r	s	t	v	y
17	16	15	14	13	12	11	10	9	8	7	6	5	4	3	2	1

(a) | 9 | 11 | 10 | 11 | 3 | 17 | 5 | 1 | = military.

(b) | 9 | 11 | 8 | 11 | 4 | 3 | 14 | 5 | = minister

(c) | 9 | 11 | 8 | 7 | 5 | 11 | 3 | 1 | = minority

(d) | 9 | 11 | 4 | 16 | 12 | 11 | 14 | 13 | = mischief

Exercise 4 — Unjumble the confused words in these sentences. Write them.

1. During a *paytilc* rainy season, that area is hit by at least four severe *onthopys*.

   (a) *typical*   (b) *typhoons.*

2. The firm made the *jaromyti* of its promotions based mainly on *neiryisot*.

   (a) *majority .*   (b) *seniority*

3. The *sinitrmy* of defence is in solve charge of *latriimy* operations in the area.

   (a) *ministry..*   (b) *military.*

4. His science test included a request to describe the *clasiyph* properties of a *drinclye*

   (a) *physical*   (b) *cylinder.*

Exercise 5 — These words are chopped up. Sort and write them.

typ	giene	= (a)	typist
ny	or	= (b)	*nylon*
hy	nus	= (c)	*hygiene*
mi	ior	= (d)	*minus,*
sen	ide	= (e)	*senior*
re	ist	= (f)	*revise*
min	vise	= (g)	*minor,*
div	lon	= (h)	*divide*

$$48 \div 8 = 6$$

Exercise 6 — Fill each bubble with an associated word from **blocks 57** to **60**.

(a) exercise   *minuscule* *physicle*

(b) study   *revise*

(c) naughtiness   *mischief*

(d) army   *military*

(e) gas   *radon*

(f) cleanliness   *hygine*

(g) material   *nylon*

(h) keyboard   *type / typewriter*

tion | ve | tion | ion | mar | re | rap

Block

61
- mystery
- mysterious
- solve
- dissolve
- solution
- revolve
- revolution

62
- region
- legion — *large military force.*
- station
- legend
- legendary
- register
- election

63
- margin
- marginal
- margarine
- language
- landscape
- horizon
- horizontal

64
- reflect
- reflection
- refund
- refreshment
- refurbish — *redecorate.*
- rapid
- rapidly

Bonus
1. _____
2. _____

Exercise 1
Write an associated **block** word for each of the following words.

(a) answer _solution_

(b) myth _legend_

(c) edge _region_

(d) work out _solve_

(e) quick _rapid_

(f) image _landscape_

(g) melt _dissolve_

(h) puzzle _mystery_

Exercise 2 Alphabetical Order
List the eight **block** words ending in -**on** from **blocks 61** to **64** in column **A**.
Then sort them alphabetically in column **B**.

a b c d e f g h i j k l m n o p q r s t u v w x y z

A list

1. solution
2. revolution
3. region
4. legion
5. station
6. election
7. horizon
8. reflection.

Alpha**B**etical list

1. election
2. horizon
3. legion
4. reflection
5. region
6. revolution
7. solution
8. station

Exercise 3 Complete these sentences using **block** words.

(a) Pele is a footballing _station_ from Brazil. This makes him a _legendary_ figure. _legend_

(b) You cannot vote in an _election_ unless you are on the _register_ of electors.

(c) If you get your money back it's called a _refund_, but if you see your image back in a piece of glass it's called a _reflection._

(d) The detectives were unable to _solve_ the crime so the identity of the killer remains a _mystery._

Exercise 4 Locate the twenty **block** words in this **wordsearch**.
Write them in the grid below as you find them.
The words are written →, ←, ↑ or ↓.

r	e	t	n	e	m	h	s	e	r	f	e	r	r	e
m	y	s	t	e	r	i	o	u	s	l	a	n	d	r
b	j	o	h	n	l	e	g	e	n	n	o	n	n	a
e	r	l	d	i	s	s	o	l	v	e	a	l	l	p
a	e	v	n	m	a	r	g	a	r	i	n	e	y	i
t	f	e	e	n	u	r	e	v	o	l	v	e	o	d
l	l	e	g	e	d	i	e	g	a	u	g	n	a	l
l	e	g	e	n	d	a	r	y	s	s	l	u	v	y
e	c	i	l	n	n	s	o	l	u	t	i	o	n	y
r	t	r	r	o	g	o	g	e	o	a	r	g	e	r
i	r	a	t	i	h	a	n	o	i	t	c	e	l	e
n	g	o	s	g	r	r	n	o	z	i	r	o	h	l
d	n	u	f	e	r	i	s	o	n	o	p	a	u	s
l	m	m	a	r	g	i	n	a	l	n	m	a	n	y
c	c	a	r	n	o	i	g	e	l	t	n	e	y	m

Write the words.

1. language
2. horizon
3. solve
4. marginal
5. dissolve
6. margarine
7. legendary
8. solution
9. revolve
10. refreshment
11. mysterious
12. reflect
13. legend
14. rapidly
15. legion
16. election
17. region
18. station
19. refund
20. mystery

Exercise 5 Use **block** words containing **re** to complete these sentences.

Example: refund

(a) We took the faulty goods back and demanded a refund.

(b) Use of the guillotine was a common method of execution during the French
revolution.

(c) Some classes moved into prefabs while the builders came in to refurbish
the classrooms.

(d) A mirror can be used to reflect the rays of the sun.

(e) 'This entire region is in danger of flooding,' warned the environmentalist.

(f) It is important to check the refreshment register of electors to make sure that
you are entitled to vote.

39

per | por | pro | pre

Block

65
agent
ancient
ocean
obese
obesity
special
especially

66
perfect
perfection
person
personal
peruse—*very careful*
popular
population

67
portion
proportion
portable
portrait
promotion
profession—*u work as.*
professor

68
portcullis
history
historical
prehistoric
previous
preview
private

Bonus
1. _____
2. _____

Exercise 1   Dictionary Work
Write the **block** words that match these definitions.

(a) large body of seawater — ~~portcullis~~ ocean.
(b) to read carefully — obese. ✗
(c) unhealthily overweight — ? obeseity
(d) a serving of food — portion. ✓
(e) a college lecturer — portcullis. ✗
(f) secure gate in castle — peruse. ✗ portcullis
(g) time before recorded history — prehistoric. ✓
(h) 007 – licensed to kill — a special ~~?~~ agent ✓
(i) an advance showing — preview ✓

Exercise 2   Alphabetical Order
List seven words ending in **n** from **blocks 66** to **68** in column **A**. Sort them alphabetically in column **B**.

a b c d e f g h i j k l m n o p q r s t u v w x y z

A list
1. perfection ✓
2. population ✓
3. portion ✓
4. proportion ✓
5. promotion ✓
6. profession ✓
7. person ✓

Alpha**B**etical list
1. perfection ✓
2. person
3. population
4. portion
5. profession
6. promotion
7. proportion

Exercise 3   Thesaurus Work
Complete these word groups using **block** words.

(a) old; time-worn; antique; — ancient
(b) image; likeness; portrayal; — portrait
(c) compact; handy; movable; — portable
(d) accepted; favoured; liked; — special ✗ popular
(e) factual; chronicled; documented; — historical ✗ histor
(f) bit; fraction; piece; — portion ✓

Exercise 4 Prefixes

Use **block** words beginning with the prefixes **por-, per-, pro-** or **pre-** to complete these sentences.

(a) The solicitor advised his client to _preview_ _preuse_ the contract before signing.

(b) The car was in good condition considering that it had two _previous_ owners.

(c) The celebrated artist was best known for his _portrait_ pictures.

(d) Music is readily available to all people now through a number of _portable_ devices.

(e) We were invited by a friend to a _preview_ of the latest James Bond movie.

(f) Many film stars use _personal_ trainers in their pursuit of the _perfect_ body.

(g) The eminent _professor_ was keen to keep his _personal_ life private.

(h) Something is said to be _prehistory_ if it was in the time before written history began.

Exercise 5 Complete these sentences using **block** words.

(a) Poor diet and lack of exercise has led to a rise in cases of _a_____.

(b) The _Ancient_ city of Rome was founded by Romulus and Remus according to legend.

(c) A prize of €100 was divided between the two children in _proportion_ to their ages.

(d) Traffic out of the city is generally heavy but can be _especially_ so at the holiday weekend.

(e) Sergeant Shanahan was rewarded for his loyalty by _promotion_ to the position of second-in-command in the army.

(f) Did you know that vinegar is often used as an effective cleaning _agent_.

(g) Cleopatra is an _ancient_ character from Egypt who died from the venomous bite of a snake.

(h) In the _previous_ sentence we could also have mentioned that she bathed only in baths of milk.

(i) A _portcullis_ was a wooden or iron grating lowered to protect the entrance to a castle.

(j) The young girl asked for a small _portion_ of cabbage.

pr   ma   un   al   ick

Block

69 prim**ary**
secon**dary**
prison
prisoner
pretty
privil**ege** — *pleasure "*
prem**ium**

70 mater**ial**
mat**tress**
ma**rathon**
Greece
Greek
marmal**ade**
mathematics

71 understand
underneath
unusual
us**ually**
a**nnual**
a**ctual**
punct**ual**

72 per**haps**
profession**al**
dial
taxi
trial
ticket
picket — *strikers.*

Bonus

1. _____
2. _____

Exercise 1 — Use **block** words to solve the clues. Write the words.

(a) another word for a jail — *prison*

(b) a person who is in jail — *prisoner*

(c) handsome or attractive — *pretty*

(d) paid to an insurance firm — *premium*

(e) you are in this type of school — *Primary*

(f) you will move to this type of school later — *Secondary*

(g) to have the honour or... — *privilege*

(h) Athens is the capital of... — *Greece*

(i) the study of numbers — *mathematics*

(j) a 26-mile race — *marathon*

Exercise 2 — Write the **block** words that contain these smaller words. Some words may appear more than once.

(a) leg — *privilege*

(b) rat — *marathon*

(c) arm — *marmalade*

(d) rim — *primary*

(e) son — *prison / prisoner*

(f) hem — *mathematics*

(g) mat — *mathematics* *mattress*

(h) and — *understand*

(i) act — *actual*

(j) eat — *underneath*

Exercise 3 — Write the **block** words that end with **al**.

(a) we would make a nice pair of curtains from this — *material*

(b) this is certainly out of the ordinary — *unusual*

(c) to get a taxi, pick up the phone and... — *dial*

(d) this meeting is only held once a year — *annual*

(e) you are on time if you are this — *punctual*

(f) usually held in court — *trial*

(g) you mean this is the very one — *actual*

(h) this person gets paid to play ball — *professional*

Exercise 4 Write the correct **block** word under each picture.

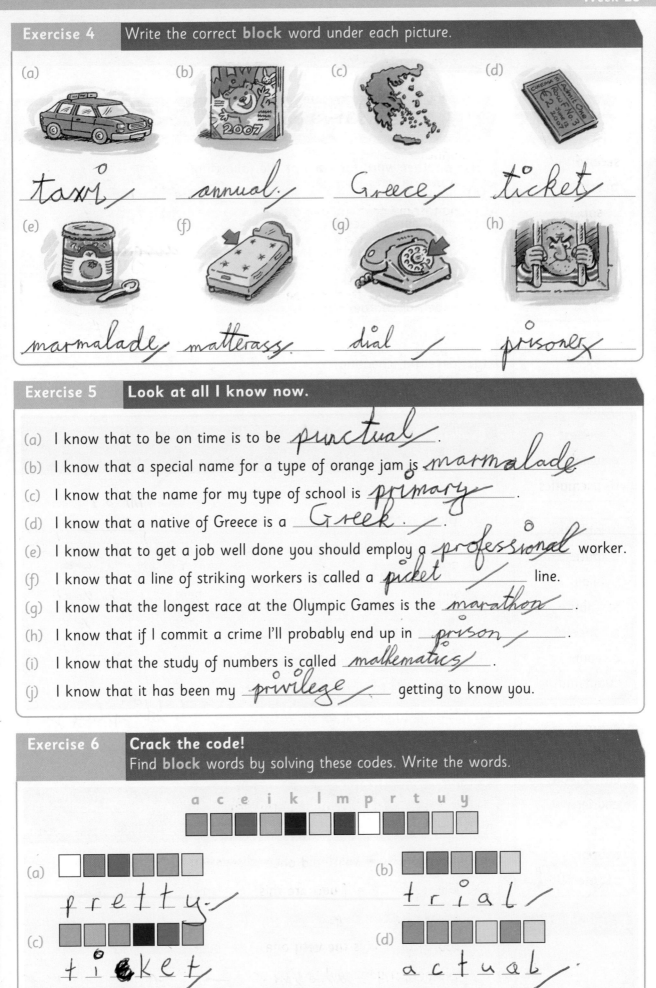

(a) *taxi*

(b) *annual*

(c) *Greece*

(d) *tickets*

(e) *marmalade*

(f) *matterass*

(g) *dial*

(h) *prisoner*

Exercise 5 Look at all I know now.

(a) I know that to be on time is to be *punctual*.

(b) I know that a special name for a type of orange jam is *marmalade*.

(c) I know that the name for my type of school is *primary*.

(d) I know that a native of Greece is a *Greek*.

(e) I know that to get a job well done you should employ a *professional* worker.

(f) I know that a line of striking workers is called a *picket* line.

(g) I know that the longest race at the Olympic Games is the *marathon*.

(h) I know that if I commit a crime I'll probably end up in *prison*.

(i) I know that the study of numbers is called *mathematics*.

(j) I know that it has been my *privilege* getting to know you.

Exercise 6 Crack the code!
Find **block** words by solving these codes. Write the words.

a c e i k l m p r t u y

(a) *pretty*

(b) *trial*

(c) *ticket*

(d) *actual*

43

ui	dis	age	ou	ous

Block

73
ruin
fluid
build
druid
builder
nuisance
disguise

74
discuss
discussion
dislike
dismiss
dishonest
disaster
disastrous

75
disabled
dispute
display
distribute
disappoint
discourage
disadvantage

76
country
courage
courageous
courier
couple
coupon
counterfeit-*fake.*

Bonus

1. _____
2. _____

Exercise 1   Thesaurus Work
Complete these word groups using **block** words.

Give another word for each of the following.

(a) liquid; flowing;   *fluid*

(b) allot; spread; scatter;   *distribute*

(c) destroy; wreck; damage;   *ruin*

(d) camouflage; mask;   *disguise*

(e) expel; discharge; remove;   *dismiss*

(f) construct; erect;   *build*

(g) deceitful; cheating;   *dishonest*

(h) pest; difficulty; annoyance;   *nuisance*

Exercise 2   Analogies
Use **block** words to complete these analogies.

Example: Niece is to aunt as nephew is to uncle

(a) Block is to solid as water is to…   *fluid*

(b) Like is to dislike as honest is to…   *dishonest*

(c) One is to two as single is to…   *couple*

(d) Real is to genuine as fake is to…   *counterfeit*

(e) Urban is to city as rural is to…   *country*

(f) Fear is to cowardice as bravery is to…   *courageous*

(g) Consent is to agree as argue is to…   *dispute*

(h) Hide is to conceal as show is to…   *display*

(i) Praise is to encourage as criticise is to… *discourage*

Exercise 3   Prefixes
Add the prefixes **cou-** or **dis-** to these jumbled letters to form **8 block** words.

Example: usnciso = cussion + dis = discussion

(a) kile   (b) tuep   (c) lep   (d) elabd
    dislike   *dispute*   *couple*   *disabled*

(e) rnyt   (f) reast   (g) gear   (h) erri
    country   *disaster*   *courage*   *courier*

Exercise 4   **Antonyms**
Write **block** words with opposite meanings to each of these words.

(a) please (**bl 75**) _disappoint_   (b) cowardly (**bl 76**) _courageous_

(c) fear (**bl 76**) ~~cour~~ _courage_   (d) advantage (**bl 75**) _disadvantage_

(e) like (**bl 74**) _dislike_   (f) genuine (**bl 76**) _counterfeit_

(g) demolish (**bl 73**) _to builds_   (h) honest (**bl 74**) _dishonest_

(i) agree (**bl 75**) _dispute_   (j) encourage (**bl 75**) _discourage_

Exercise 5   Write the missing **block** words to complete this **Sports Report**.

Following a lengthy _build_ the committee decided to _dismiss_ the coach of the National team.

This followed a series of _conterfeit_ results and a _druid_ with some of the leading players. The Chairman wanted to state that while he didn't _dislike_ the coach as a person, it would be _nuisance_ to

say that there had not been a serious difference of opinion between them.

It would now appear that the chances of our qualifying for the world tug-of-war

championships lie in _dishonest.._ or are quite slim.

Exercise 6   **Crack the code!**
Find **block** words by solving these codes. Write the words.

a	b	c	d	e	f	g	h	i	n	o	r	s	t	u	y
16	15	14	13	12	11	10	9	8	7	6	5	4	3	2	1

(a) 13 5 2 8 13 = _druid_

(b) 13 8 4 16 4 3 5 6 2 4 = _disastrous_

(c) 13 8 4 14 2 4 4 = _discuss._

(d) 7 2 8 4 16 7 14 12 = _nuisance_

(e) 14 6 2 7 3 5 1 = _country._

(f) 13 8 4 9 6 7 12 4 3 = _dishonest_

(g) 14 6 2 7 3 12 5 11 12 8 3 = _counterfeit._

(h) 14 6 2 5 16 10 12 = _courage._ 23/02/18

| con | cat | col | gi | double letters |

Block

77 conscience
conscious
unconscious
hospital
ambulance
cemetery
ceremony

78 certificate
century
centenary
category
catalogue
caterpillar
cathedral

79 collide
collision
collapse
collection
collar
colleague
recollect

80 giant
gigantic
giraffe
ginger
gimmick
giggle
gipsy

Bonus

1. _____
2. _____

Exercise 1

Use every alternate letter to discover the eight **block** words in the **wordsnake**. Write the words.
There are 4 words in red and 4 words in black.

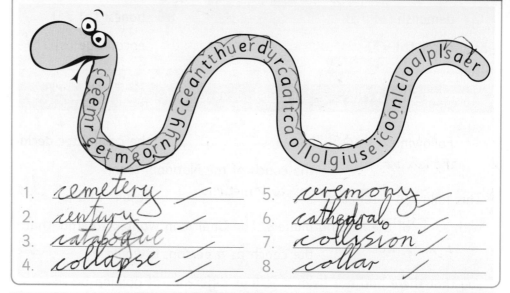

1. cemetery
2. century
3. catalogue
4. collapse
5. ceremony
6. cathedral
7. collision
8. collar

Exercise 2

Fill in the boxes with letters that fit their shape from **blocks 77** to **80**.

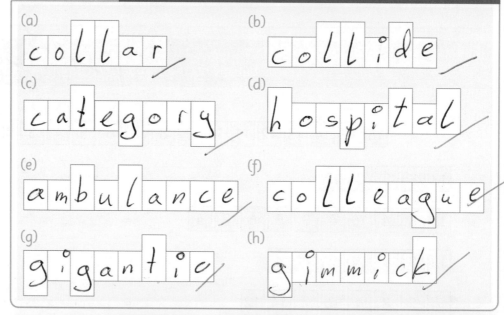

(a) collar
(b) collide
(c) category
(d) hospital
(e) ambulance
(f) colleague
(g) gigantic
(h) gimmick

Exercise 3

These **block** words have been mixed up. Sort them out and write them correctly.

(a) collaffe — collide
(b) hosger — hospital x
(c) cathemony — cathedral
(d) girpital — giraffe
(e) certury — ceremony
(f) censcious — century
(g) conide — conscious
(h) ginedral — ginger

46

Exercise 4 There are **11 block** words that contain a double letter.
Find and write them.

1. caterpillar
2. collide
3. collision
4. collapse
5. collection
6. collar
7. colleague
8. recollect
9. giraffe
10. gimmick
11. giggle

Exercise 5 **Dictionary Work**
Write the **block** words that match these dictionary definitions.

(a) to fall down suddenly — collapse

(b) the larva of a butterfly — caterpillar

(c) a trick to draw attention to something — gimmick

(d) to crash violently — unconscious

(e) a fellow worker — colleague

(f) the chief church of a diocese — cathedral

(g) a place to treat ill people — hospital

(h) an organised list of goods for sale — catalogue

Exercise 6 **Alphabetical Order**
List all the **block** words from **blocks 78** and **79** that begin with the
letter **c** in column **A**. Then sort them alphabetically in column **B**.

A list

1. collision.
2. collide
3. collection.
4. colleague
5. collar
6. collapse
7. certificate
8. century
9. centenary
10. cathedral
11. caterpillar
12. category
13. catalouge

AlphaBetical list

1. catalouge
2. category
3. caterpillar
4. cathedral
5. centenary
6. century
7. certificate
8. collapse
9. collar
10. colleague
11. collection
12. collide
13. collision

13/03/18

| mag | ic | ly | app | for | ate | eign |

Block

81 Belgium
magic
magician
tragic
tragedy
basic
basically

82 appetite
appointment
application
appreciate
appreciation
apprentice
applicant

83 approve
approval
approach
approximately
appliance
applaud
applause

84 fortune
fortunate
unfortunate
unfortunately
fortnight
foreign
foreigner

Bonus

1. _____
2. _____

Exercise 1 — Dictionary Work

Write the **block** words that match these definitions.

(a) a desire for food — *appetite*

(b) uses tricks to create illusions — *magician*

(c) home to fine lace and chocolate — *Belgium*

(d) a person learning a trade — *apprentice*

(e) date with a doctor — *appointment*

(f) request for a job — *application*

(g) happening of great sorrow — *tragedy*

(h) person applying for a job — *appliance* / *applicant*

Exercise 2

Unscramble the confused words in these sentences. Write them.

(a) The audience was amazed at the tricks of the gamicnia. — *magician*

(b) A gift of flowers is a nice way to show that you partapeice somebody. — *appreciate*

(c) The council imposed a charge for the disposal of the electrical panipalec. — *appliance*

(d) Dermot won the raffle but fuatelnnotury he couldn't find his winning ticket. — *unfortunately*

(e) That dangerous junction has been the scene of many garitc accidents. — *tragic*

(f) The young girl had ambitions to travel to many rogifen countries. — *foreign*

Exercise 3 — Synonyms

Write an associated **block** word for each of these words.

(a) lucky — *fortunate*   (b) sorcery — *magic*

(c) clap — *applause*   (d) device — *appliance*

(e) gratitude — *appreciation*   (f) riches — *fortune*

(g) candidate — *applicant*   (h) catastrophe — *unfortunately* tra

(i) minimal — *basic*   (j) trainee — *apprentice*

Exercise 4   Crack the code!

Find **block** words by solving these codes. Write the words.

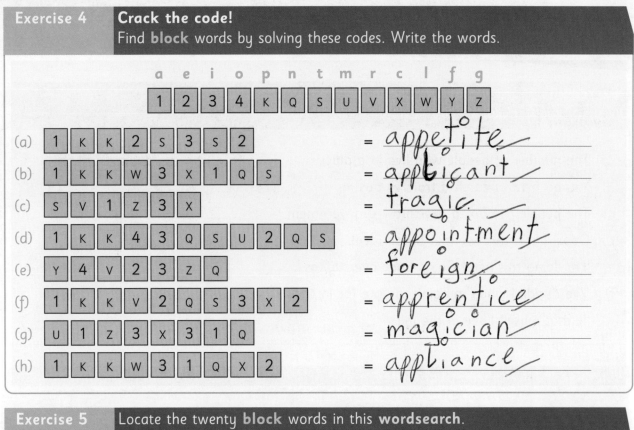

a	e	i	o	p	n	t	m	r	c	l	f	g
1	2	3	4	K	Q	S	U	V	X	W	Y	Z

(a) `1 K K 2 S 3 S 2` = appetite

(b) `1 K K W 3 X 1 Q S` = applicant

(c) `S V 1 Z 3 X` = tragic

(d) `1 K K 4 3 Q S U 2 Q S` = appointment

(e) `Y 4 V 2 3 Z Q` = foreign

(f) `1 K K V 2 Q S 3 X 2` = apprentice

(g) `U 1 Z 3 X 3 1 Q` = magician

(h) `1 K K W 3 1 Q X 2` = appliance

Exercise 5

Locate the twenty **block** words in this **wordsearch**.
Enter them in the spaces provided below as you find them.
The words are written →, ←, ↑ or ↓.

a	p	p	l	a	u	s	e	n	g	i	e	r	o	f
p	r	o	f	o	r	t	b	a	s	i	c	i	c	s
p	o	f	o	r	t	u	n	n	e	e	n	u	b	b
l	f	o	r	t	u	n	e	b	a	s	a	i	c	a
i	m	r	t	a	e	n	g	i	c	b	i	a	i	s
c	u	t	u	e	t	e	n	a	i	a	l	p	s	i
a	n	n	n	t	i	h	c	a	o	r	p	p	a	c
t	a	i	a	a	t	n	f	o	r	e	p	r	p	a
i	i	g	t	i	e	q	n	u	t	n	a	e	p	l
o	c	h	e	c	p	t	e	l	y	g	q	n	l	l
n	i	t	p	e	p	t	r	a	g	i	c	t	i	y
p	g	r	t	r	a	g	e	d	y	e	o	i	c	q
p	a	a	p	p	l	a	u	d	a	r	h	c	a	c
p	m	l	i	p	c	a	n	t	a	o	p	e	n	p
a	a	e	t	a	n	u	t	r	o	f	n	u	t	l

Write the words.

1. foreign
2. fortunate
3. fortnight
4. application
5. applause
6. basic
7. basically
8. tragedy
9. tragic
10. applaud
11. unfortunate
12. fortune
13. apprentice
14. appliance
15. approach
16. applicant
17. appreciate
18. appetite
19. foreigner
20. magic

13/05/18

Exercise 1 Use words that end in -**in** or -**ion** from **blocks 57** to **84** to solve these clues. Write the words.

(a) The number of people who live in a place. _____

(b) You go here to catch a train or bus. _____

(c) The people rise up to overthrow a government. _____

(d) Oops! Looks like we met by accident. _____

(e) 'I'm doing this here! Going back over things.' _____

(f) 'I've decided who I'm going to vote for in the...' _____

(g) 'Is that myself I see in the mirror?' _____

Exercise 2 **Alphabetical Order**
There are 19 words that end in -**y** to be found between **blocks 65** and **84**. List the words in column **A**. Then sort them alphabetically in column **B**.

A list

1. _____
2. _____
3. _____
4. _____
5. _____
6. _____
7. _____
8. _____
9. _____
10. _____
11. _____
12. _____
13. _____
14. _____
15. _____
16. _____
17. _____
18. _____
19. _____

Alpha**B**etical list

1. a _ _ _ _ _ _ _ _ _ _ _
2. _ _ _ _ _ _ _ _ _ _
3. _ _ _ _ _ _ _ _ _
4. _ _ m _ _ _ _ _
5. _ _ _ _ _ _ _ _
6. _ _ _ t _ _ _ _
7. _ _ _ _ _ _ _
8. _ _ _ _ _ _ _
9. _ _ _ _ _ _ _
10. _ _ _ _ _ _ _ _ _
11. _ _ _ _ _
12. _ _ s _ _ _ _
13. _ _ _ _ _ _ _
14. _ _ e _ _ _
15. _ _ _ _ _ _
16. _ _ _ _ _ _ _
17. _ r _ _ _ _
18. _ _ _ _ _ _ _ _ _ _
19. _ _ u _ _ _ _

Exercise 3 — Analogies
Use words from **blocks 57** to **84** to help you complete these analogies.

(a) alike is to dislike as honest is to... _____

(b) teacher is to school as nurse is to... _____

(c) Berlin is to Germany as Brussels is to... _____

(d) jam is to bread as _____?_____ is to toast... _____

(e) remove is to removal as approve is to... _____

(f) 10 is to decade as 100 is to... _____

(g) plumber is to trade as doctor is to... _____

(h) lucky is to fortunate as unlucky is to... _____

(i) Dutch is to Holland as Greek is to... _____

(j) rivers are to Geography as dates are to... _____

Exercise 4 — Missing person alert!
Locate these people from the **blocks** indicated below.

(a) was locked up awaiting trial: (**bl 69**) _____

(b) is someone I work with: (**bl 79**) _____

(c) works in secret for the government: (**bl 65**) _____

(d) amazed us with his tricks: (**bl 81**) _____

(e) a native of Greece: (**bl 70**) _____

(f) a person who delivers parcels: (**bl 76**) _____

(g) actually gets paid for playing sport: (**bl 72**) _____

(h) applied for a job here: (**bl 82**) _____

(i) this person just annoys me: (**bl 73**) _____

(j) two for the price of one with this pair: (**bl 76**) _____

Exercise 5 — Antonyms
Write words opposite in meaning to these **words** from the **blocks** indicated below.

(a) multiplication (**bl 60**) _____   (b) modern (**bl 65**) _____

(c) relegation (**bl 67**) _____   (d) ugly (**bl 69**) _____

(e) sprint (**bl 70**) _____   (f) usual (**bl 71**) _____

(g) amateur (**bl 72**) _____   (h) honest (**bl 74**) _____

(i) conscious (**bl 77**) _____   (j) dwarf (**bl 80**) _____

(k) exactly (**bl 83**) _____   (l) native (**bl 84**) _____

| sci | ce | car | au | tion | ea | ure |

Block

85 science
scientist
scientific
scissors
accept
access
accent

86 carve
carvery
caravan
carol
carpenter
carbon
cardboard

87 cautious
caution
precaution — action to prevent something bad from happening
cauldron
fault
default
vault

88 feature
creature
torture
lecture
figure
literature
temperature

Bonus

1. _____
2. _____

Exercise 1   Complete these sentences using **block** words.

(a) 'It gives me great pleasure to _accept_ this cup.'

(b) Paper, _scissors_, stone is an amusing game.

(c) You can tell where someone comes from at times by listening to their _accent_.

(d) A dentist works in a surgery but a _scientist_ works in a laboratory.

(e) The investigator needed to have _access_ to all the files in order to complete his report.

(f) It is a _scientific_ fact that water boils at 100°C.

(g) We had to call a _carpenter_ to come and fix the broken stairway.

(h) I must concentrate hard and remember to put the 'd' between car and board in _cardboard_.

Exercise 2   Dictionary Work
Write the **block** words that match these definitions.

(a) song sung at Christmas — _carol_

(b) safe area in a bank — _vault_

(c) measure of hot and cold — _temperature_

(d) a witch's large pot — _cauldron_

(e) cutting instrument — _scissors_

(f) to cut in slices — _carve_

(g) action taken to avoid trouble — _caution_

(h) talk given by a professor — _lecture_

(i) books and writings — _literature_

Exercise 3   Unscramble these letters to make **block** words.

e e s i
n c c

u e t u
i o u s

t t i r r
u v a e

science   _cautious_   _literature_

Exercise 4 Rhyming Words

Complete these groups of rhyming words with **block** words.

(a) argum**ent**; obedi**ent**; _accent_

(b) artist; dentist; _scientist_

(c) neon; radon; _cauldron_

(d) petrol; alcohol; _carol_

(e) character; messenger; _carpenter_

(f) conscious; spacious; _cautious_

(g) delivery; jewellery; _carvery_.

(h) except; slept; _accept_

Exercise 5 These words are chopped up. Sort and write them.

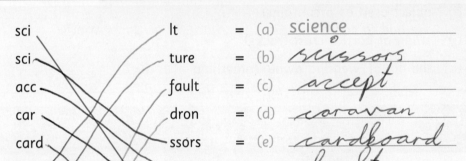

sci	lt	= (a) _science_
sci	ture	= (b) _scissors_
acc	fault	= (c) _accept_
car	dron	= (d) _caravan_
card	ssors	= (e) _cardboard_
fau	ept	= (f) _fault_
fea	avan	= (g) _feature_
fig	ence	= (h) _figure_
caul	board	= (i) _cauldron_
de	ure	= (j) _default_.

Exercise 6 Complete these sentences using **block** words.

The published _scientist_ invited _science_ students from her university
to a _lecture_ where the eminent _scientist_ Dr. Windup was about to
announce his latest _scientific_ discovery.

A unique _feature_ (vd) of his most recent experiments was the conversion of
carbon -dioxide back to oxygen by reducing the _temperature_ to a previously
unknown _figure_.

As always with Dr. Windup, the advice to students would be, 'Proceed with
caution!'

pe | y | double letters | sion | ess | geo

Block

89
pedal
pedestrian
petrol
penalty
penance
percentage
percussion

90
hidden
forbidden
dagger
gallery
stubborn
fiddle
vessel

91
fitness
witness
confess
passage
impossible
impression
impressive

92
geology
geography
geometry
erosion
excursion
vision
television

Bonus

1. _____
2. _____

Exercise 1 — Dictionary Work

Write the **block** words that match these definitions.

(a) fuel for non-diesel car engines — *petrol*

(b) person walking — *pedestrian*

(c) section of orchestra containing drums

(d) marked out of 100 — *percentage*

(e) awarded for a foul in penalty area (soccer)

(f) exhibition area for artists' work

(g) musical instrument like violin

(h) quality of being obstinate

(i) object used as a container

(j) study of Earth's crust (rocks)

(k) the act of 'wearing away' something

Absent

Exercise 2

Write the **two** words that need to be exchanged in order to complete each sentence.

Example: The hidden city is a forbidden jewel in the Chinese city of Beijing.

The <u>forbidden</u> city is a <u>hidden</u> jewel in the Chinese city of Beijing.

(a) The motorist had to hit the pedestrian hard in order to avoid knocking down the pedal.

(i) _____ (ii) _____

(b) The accused stubbornly refused to witness to the crime even though the police had an eye-confess account.

(i) _____ (ii) _____

(c) Brutus killed Julius Caesar with a hidden, which he had dagger in his toga.

(i) _____ (ii) _____

(d) The erosion class went on a field trip to see examples of geography on the coast.

(i) _____ (ii) _____

(e) I can never figure out whether it is geography or geology that is part of the geometry lesson.

(i) _____ (ii) _____

Exercise 3 — Analogies

Use **block** words to complete these analogies.

(a) Oar is to boat as _pedal_ is to bike.

(b) Quiver is to arrows as sheath is to ~~impossible~~ _vessel_

(c) 'Yes' is to possible as 'no' is to _impossible_.

(d) Audio is to radio as vision is to _____.

(e) Library is to books as _gallery_ is to paintings.

(f) Strong is to horse as _____ is to mule.

(g) Road is to motorist as footpath is to _pedestrian_.

(h) Mouth is to tin whistle as hand is to _fiddle_.

(i) Lorry is to diesel as _petrol_ is to car.

Exercise 4

Write the correct **block** word under each picture.

(a) _percentage_

(b) _television_

(c) _fiddle_

(d) _____

(e) _pedal_

(f) _dagger_

(g) _____

(h) _geometry_

Exercise 5

Make as many words as you can using the letters from the word **percentage**. All words must have a minimum of 4 letters.

1. _cent_
2. _cage_
3. _cane_
4. _tape_
5. _tree_
6. _rent_
7. _teen_
8. _agent_
9. _trace_
10. _grant_
11. _carpet_
12. _centre_
13. _percent_
14. _teenager_
15. _generate_
16. _acre_
17. _earn_
18. _neat_
19. _gate_
20. _rate_ .

imm | in | al | ea | ure | for

Block

93 immediate
immediately
immortal
immense -huge
immerse
immune
implement

94 index
individual f.o.
industry
industrial
mammal
musical
cymbal

95 frequent
frequently
frequency
measure
pleasure
pleasant
treasure

96 former
formation
information
formula
formal
forty
forward

Bonus

1. _____
2. _____

Exercise 1   Replace the words in brackets with words taken from **blocks 93** and **94**.

(a) This new law will come into force with (straight away) effect.

immediate ✓

(b) We checked the (list of contents) at the back of the book to see if the item was listed.

index ✓

(c) It was believed that some of the Greek Gods were (could live for ever).

immortal ✓

(d) The (factories) estate is convenient to all major routes.

~~formal~~ *formation* ✗

(e) A rough working (tool) was unearthed by the archaeologist.

implement ✗

(f) An (made for one) training schedule was designed for each athlete.

individual ✓

(g) The traveller had to receive a vaccination to keep her (protected) from infection by malaria.

immune ✓

(h) In order to test for leaks, we had to (put deep in liquid) the tube in water.

immerse ✓

(i) The (percussion instrument) was struck hard by the percussionist.

cymbal

Exercise 2   Separate the words from **blocks 95** and **96** according to the amount of syllables they have.

two syllables	**three** syllables	**four** syllables
fre / quent ✓	fre / quent / ly ✓	in / for / ma / tion ✓
mea / sure ✓	fre / quen / cy ✓	
plea / sure ✓	for / ma / tion ✓	
plea / sant ✓	for / mu / la ✓	
trea / sure ✓		
for / mer ✓		
for / mal ✓		
for / ty ✓		
for / ward ✓		

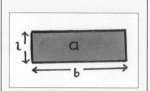

Exercise 3 — Al here again.
Use **block** words ending with **al** to solve these unusual clues.

(a) Are you here as your own person? — *individual*

(b) So you reckon you're going to live forever. — *immortal*

(c) You are this kind of animal. — *mammal*

(d) This type of worker works in a factory. — ~~formal~~ *industrial* / ~~pass~~ ~~industrial~~ *informal*

(e) What a sweet voice you've got. —

(f) I see you play a percussion instrument. — *cymbal*

(g) Mr Al, don't you look great in your dress suit. — *formal*

Exercise 4
Unjumble the confused words in these sentences. Write them.

(a) The east coast of America is uetqnylfer hit by tornadoes. — *frequently*

(b) The recipe or rumofal for Coca-cola is a closely guarded secret. — *formula*

(c) The gangster thought that he was nuemim from prosecution by the law. — *immune*

(d) Is a whale a malamm or a fish? — *mammal*

(e) We enjoyed a tapelasn day out at the beach. — *pleasant*

(f) The specialist air-corps team practised their mortifano flying endlessly. — *information*

(g) Many coastal resorts were hit by an senemim tsunami following the earthquake. — *immense*

(h) Captain Hook sailed the seven seas in search of suartere to plunder. — *treasure*

(i) I prefer to play as a arfowdr than as a back in a football game. — *forward*

(j) The guitar is my favourite sacmuil instrument. — *musical*

Exercise 5 — Synonyms
Write an associated **block** word for each of the following.

(a) previous — *former*

(b) instant — *immediately ?*

(c) everlasting — *immortal ?*

(d) enjoyment —

(e) riches — *?*

(f) one person — *individual*

(g) manufacturing — *?*

(h) often — *frequent* 20/04/18.

tch | il | al | ea | ous | ious

Block

97
- di**tch**
- fe**tch**
- swi**tch**
- twi**tch**
- unt**il**
- ev**il**
- inst**all**

98
- festiv**al**
- reh**ea**rs**al**
- soci**al**
- origin**al**
- h**ea**rd
- h**ea**rse – *vehicle (for coffins)*
- h**ea**dphones

99
- nerv**ous**
- jeal**ous**
- ridicul**ous**
- tremend**ous**
- gorge**ous**
- enorm**ous**
- por**ous** – *not secure*

100
- anx**ious**
- delic**ious**
- ser**ious**
- fur**ious**
- var**ious**
- suspic**ious**
- prev**ious**

Bonus

1. _____
2. _____

Exercise 1   Use **block** words to complete each sentence.

(a) An electrician called to replace the faulty _switch_.

(b) While he was there he also managed to _install_ our new cooker.

(c) 'Jack and Jill went up the hill to _fetch_ a pail of water.'

(d) 'I'm not winking, it's just a nervous _twitch_ I have in my eye,' said the clown.

(e) Our play goes on tomorrow night but we have a full dress _rehearsal_ today.

(f) 'Have you seen the _headphones_ for my MP3 player?'

(g) 'I've _heard_ that song before and I have to say that I prefer the _original_ version,' said Mari.

(h) We had to wait _until_ the ticket-desk opened at 9am to buy tickets for the big music _festival_.

(i) My mother cooked a _delicious_ meal for us.

(j) We were all very _nervous_ before the game.

Exercise 2   Write the correct word in each sentence.

(a) An _enormous_ crowd gathered outside the store for the official opening.

(b) _Nervous_ is the adjective formed from the word nerve.

(c) You cannot be _serious_! The ball was obviously out!

(d) The bride looked absolutely _gorgeous_ on her wedding day.

(e) 'Don't pay any attention to his remarks. He's only _jealous_ that you are on the team,' said Shane.

(f) There was a _enormous_ _tremendous_ roar as each of the teams entered Croke Park.

(g) The _porous_ sponge sucked in the water.

(h) Mam was _furious_ when she saw the broken window.

Exercise 3 — Write the **block** words that contain these smaller words.

(a) gin _original_

(b) hone _headphones_

(c) or _porous_

(d) rid _rediculous_

(e) rev _previous_

(f) fur _furious_

(g) wit _twitch_

(h) men _tremendous_

Exercise 4 — ObvIOUSly I Owe U Something if you help me spell these. (**block 100**)

(a) How angry are you? _furious_

(b) Lots of choice here. _various_

(c) This is more than tasty. _delicious_

(d) Were we here before? _previous_

(e) I think you doubt my intentions. _suspicious_

(f) Why are you so worried? _anxious_

Exercise 5 — Replace the words in brackets with **block** words.

(a) This is just a (practice) for the main event. _rehearsal_

(b) Some (silly) people still believe that the Earth is flat. _ridiculous_

(c) The (envious) dictator had his opponents murdered. _jealous_

(d) There was a (huge) response to the appeal for aid. _enormous_

(e) Water can penetrate (permeable) rocks. _porous_

(f) The (funeral car) arrived to take the corpse from the hospital. _hearse_

(g) The (first) inhabitants of Australia were the Aborigines. _original_

(h) The (trench) at the side of the field was full of water. _ditch_

Exercise 6 — We're nearly at the end of this book. Look at all that I know now!

(a) I know that a plumber comes to _install_ a washing machine.

(b) I know that practising for a concert is called a _rehearsal_.

(c) I know that the first issue of anything is called an _original_.

(d) I know that an undertaker drives a _hearse_.

(e) I know that rocks that allow water through are _porous_.

(f) I know that a great racing _festival_ is held in Galway each year.

_27/04/18_

59

| de | tion | ent | ris |

Block

101
demand
demolish
democracy
democratic
demonstrate
delight
delightful

102
desperate
destination
deposit
detective
determined
depend
deprive—to take away.

103
depart
departure
department
denomination
deplete — to decrease seriously.
dependent
independent

104
depth
deputy
dense
debut — first. first appearance.
debris — wreckage. ruins.
desert
dessert

Bonus

1. _____
2. _____

Exercise 1

Six of the seven words from **block 101** are in this **wordsnake**. Read every second letter to find them. Write the words. There are 3 words in red and 3 words in black.

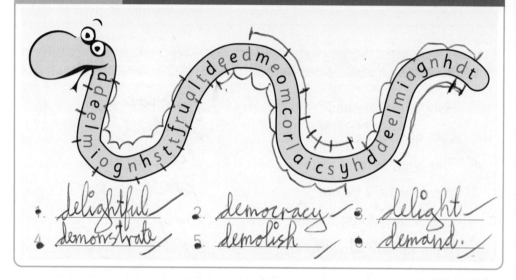

1. delightful   2. democracy   3. delight
4. demonstrate   5. demolish   6. demand

Exercise 2

Fill in the boxes with letters that fit their shape.

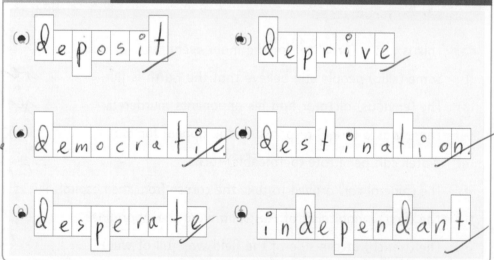

(a) deposit
(b) deprive
(c) democratic
(d) destination
(e) desperate
(f) independant

Exercise 3

Thesaurus Work
Complete these word groups using **block** words.

(a) rubble; wreckage;   debris
(b) request; insist on;   dezire to
(c) enjoyable; enchanting; delightful
(d) show; display;   demonstration
(e) leaving; going;   departure
(f) wreck; flatten;   depressi x demolish

Exercise 4 — Antonyms
Write **block** words with opposite meanings to each of these.

(a) arrival — *departure* ✓
(b) sparse — *?*
(c) build — *demolish* ✓
(d) dependent — *independent* ✓
(e) starting point — *~~destination~~*
(f) augment — *?*
(g) withdraw — *deposit* ✓
(h) undemocratic — *democratic* ✓
(i) enrich — *?*
(j) displeasing — *?*

Exercise 5 — Prefixes
Join the prefixes **dep-**, **dem-** or **des-** to these jumbled letters to form 8 **block** words. Example: **ned = end + dep = depend**.

tele	rest	tug	hosil
dan	tosi	evir	trapee

1. *deplete* ✓
2. *dessert* ✓
3. *deputy* ✓
4. *demolish* ✓
5. *demand* ✓
6. *deposit* ✓
7. *deprive* ✓
8. *desperate* ✓

Exercise 6 — Crack the code!
Find **block** words by solving these codes. Write the words.

a d e i m n o p r s t

(a) = *demand*
(b) = *depart* ✓
(c) = *depend* ✓
(d) = *dessert* ✓
(e) = *deposit* ✓
(f) = *dependent* ✓
(g) = *desperate* ✓
(h) = *determined* ✓
(i) = *denomination* ✓

| sion | pr | res | re | ei |

Block

105
Russia
passion
permission
mission
primitive —
profile
profitable

106
precise
precisely
practical
practically
impractical
precede _to go before_
pronounce

107
response
responsible
responsibility
repeat
repair
represent
require

108
seize _to take a hold of._
weird
scout
suggest
valley
hobbies
grammar

Bonus

1. _____
2. _____

Exercise 1 — Thesaurus Work

Some words may have more than one meaning depending on the context. Identify these **block** words from the clues. Write the words.

(a) a sketch or an outline — ~~profile~~ profile

(b) ancient or undeveloped — ~~precede~~ primitive.

(c) useful or sensible — responsible

(d) gone before or lead up to — valley

(e) to say again or duplicate — repeat

(f) a reaction or reply — response

(g) a task or a delegation — mission. ~~responsibility~~

(h) to grab hold of or confiscate — seize

(i) a duty or reliability — mission

(j) moneymaking or useful — profitable

(k) to compel or need — require

Exercise 2

Unscramble the confused words in these sentences. Write the sentences.

(a) She asked for ~~simpresoni~~ to close the blinds.

She asked for permission to close the blinds.

(b) 'I now ~~nocropune~~ you man and wife,' said the preacher.

'I now pronounce you man and wife,' said the preacher.

(c) We ~~quierer~~ that you wash your hands before entering the ward.

We require that you wash your hands before entering the ward.

(d) The ~~toucs~~ was able to report that the Apaches had gathered in the ~~lavyel~~.

The scout was able to report that the Apaches had ga the in the valley.

(e) They were on a ~~somnisi~~ deep in the Amazon in search of ~~viperitim~~ tribes.

They were on a mission deep in the Amazon in search of primitive tribes.

(f) Some ~~boshebi~~ such as oil-painting can also be quite ~~torfabepil~~ for the artist.

Some hobbies such as oil-painting can also be quite profitable for the artist.

62

Exercise 3 — Alphabetical Order

List all the words from **blocks 105** and **106** that begin with the letter **p** in column **A**. Then sort them alphabetically in column **B**.

A list
1. passion ✓
2. permission ✓
3. primitive ✓
4. profile ✓
5. profitable ✓
6. precise ✓
7. precisely ✓
8. practical ✓
9. practically ✓
10. precede ✓
11. pronounce ✓

Alpha**B**etical list
1. passion
2. permission
3. practical
4. practically
5. precede
6. precise
7. precisely
8. primitive
9. profile
10. profitable
11. pronounce

Exercise 4 — Analogies

Use **block** words to help complete these analogies.

(a) Ancient is to _primitive_ as modern is to advanced.

(b) Girl is to guide as boy is to _scout_.

(c) _permission_ is to allow as refusal is to deny.

(d) Practical is to impractical as _profitable_ is to unprofitable.

(e) Before is to after as _precede_ is to follow.

(f) Astronaut is to USA as cosmonaut is to _Russia_.

(g) Throw is to propel as catch is to _seize_.

(h) Suitable is to suitability as response is to _responsibility_

(i) Love is to lovely as precise is to _precisely_.

Exercise 5

Unscramble these letters to make **block** words.

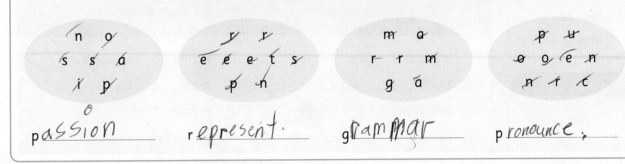

passion   represent   grammar   pronounce

week 31

double letters | y | cr | ei

Block

109
jewel
jewellery
embarrass
exaggerate
cruelly
college
balloon

110
miniature
laboratory
except
cruelty
woollen
marriage
physical

111
medicine ✓
familiar ✓
estuary ✓
curiosity ✓
neighbour ✓
permanent ✓
souvenir ✓

112
leisure ✓
enormous ✓
criticism ✓✓
burglar ✓✓
secretary ✓
receipt ✓
poisonous ✓

Bonus
1. _____
2. _____

Exercise 1   Dictionary Work
Use **block** words to solve these clues. Write them.

(a) made with gold and precious stones — jewellery ✓
(b) school, but Third Level — college ✓
(c) rises when filled with helium — balloon ✓
(d) work place of scientist — laboratory ✓
(e) anything made from wool — woollen ✓
(f) where a river joins the sea — estuary ✓
(g) person who lives next door — neighbour ✓
(h) got from the shopkeeper when you pay — receipt ✓

Exercise 2
Separate the words from **blocks 111** and **112** into the correct boxes according to the amount of syllables they have.

two syllables
neigh / bour
lei / sure ✓
bur / glar ✓
re / ceipt ✓

three syllables
med / i / cine
es / tua / ry ✓
per / man / ent ✓
sou / ven / ir ✓
en / or / mous ✓

four syllables
fam / il / i / ar
cri / ti / ci / sm ✓
se / cre / ta / ry ✓
poi / son / ou / s ✓

five syllables
cu / ri / os / i / ty ✓

Exercise 3   Synonyms
Write words similar in meaning to the following.

(a) trinkets — jewellery ✓
(b) memento — souvenir ✓
(c) thief — burglar ✓
(d) huge — enormous ✓
(e) embellish — exaggerate ✓
(f) fluster — cruelly/cruelty ✓
(g) remedy — medicine ✓
(h) university — college ✓

64

Exercise 4   Write **block** words that contain these smaller words.

(a) wool _woollen_ ✓

(b) bar _embarrass_ ✓

(c) age _marriage_ . ✓

(d) sit _curiousity_ ✓

(e) well _jewellery_ ✓

(f) our _neighbour_ ✓

(g) liar _familiar_ ✓

(h) leg _college_ ✓

(i) ball _balloon_ ✓

(j) mini _miniature_ ✓

(k) son _poisonous_ ✓

(l) mane _permanent_ ✓

Exercise 5   You'll need a double letter to solve some of these unusual clues.

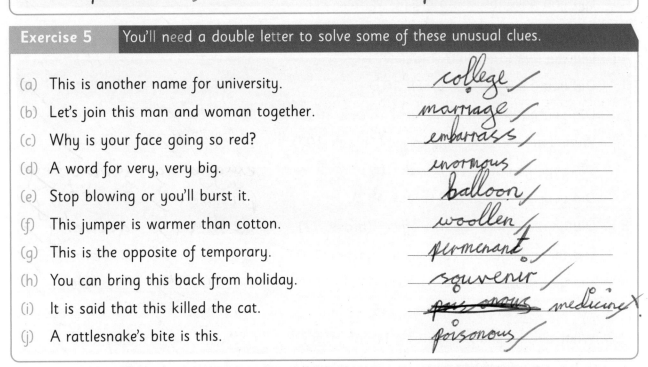

(a) This is another name for university. — _college_ ✓

(b) Let's join this man and woman together. — _marriage_ ✓

(c) Why is your face going so red? — _embarrass_ ✓

(d) A word for very, very big. — _enormous_ ✓

(e) Stop blowing or you'll burst it. — _balloon_ ✓

(f) This jumper is warmer than cotton. — _woollen_ ✓

(g) This is the opposite of temporary. — _permenant_ ✓

(h) You can bring this back from holiday. — _souvenir_ ✓

(i) It is said that this killed the cat. — ~~poisonous~~ _medicine_ ✗

(j) A rattlesnake's bite is this. — _poisonous_ ✓

Exercise 6   Fill in the boxes with letters that fit their shape.

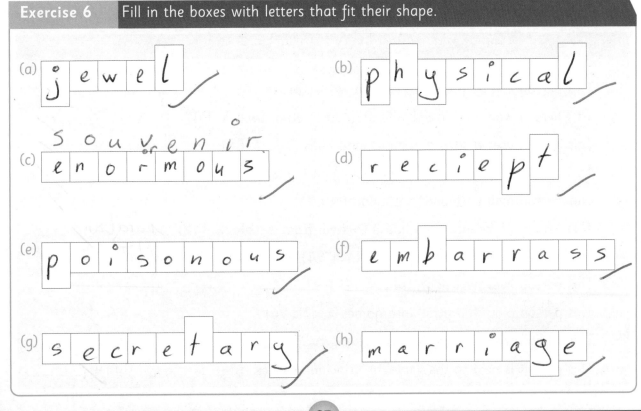

(a) j e w e l ✓

(b) p h y s i c a l ✓

(c) s o u v e n i r / e n o r m o u s ✓

(d) r e c i e p t ✓

(e) p o i s o n o u s ✓

(f) e m b a r r a s s ✓

(g) s e c r e t a r y ✓

(h) m a r r i a g e ✓

Exercise 1 Find the **block** words that contain these smaller clue words in the **blocks** mentioned.

Example: How many cent did you spend on the pet? <u>percentage</u>   <u>petrol</u>

(a) Did you eat a fig? (**block 88**)   feature ✓   figure ✓

(b) Did you have the wit to get fit? (**block 91**)   witness ✓   fitness ✓

(c) Did mam see the dust? (**block 94**)   mammal ✓   industry ✓

(d) Did the twit lose it all? (**block 97**)   twitch ✓   install ✓

(e) Did you mine for tin? (**block 102**)   determined ✓   destination ✓

(f) Did you put it back in the den? (**block 104**)   deputy ✓   dense ✓

(g) Were you sent something to eat? (**block 107**)   represent ✓   repeat ✓

(h) We hope you ate well. (**block 109**)   exaggerate ✓   jewellery ✓

(i) Did your son sit on tar? (**block 112**)   poisonous ✓   secretary ✓

(j) Did you log on to the met office? (**block 92**)   geology ✓   geometry ✓

(k) Did the man get the correct rate? (**block 101**)   demand ✓   demonstrate ✓

(l) Did you sit on our fence? (**block 111**)   curiosity ✓   neighbour ✓

(m) What age is the mini? (**block 110**)   marriage ✓   miniature ✓

(n) What did the pair eat? (**block 107**)   repair ✓   repeat ✓

Exercise 2 **Missing person alert!**
Use these clues to help find the missing person in the **blocks** mentioned.

(a) This person can be found walking to work. (**block 89**)   pedestrian ✓

(b) This person would be useful when typing a letter. (**block 112**)   secretary ✓

(c) This person uses a saw, a hammer and nails. (**block 86**)   carpenter ✓

(d) This young person should be good at tying knots. (**block 108**)   scout ✓

(e) This person may be found in a laboratory. (**block 85**)   scientist ✓

(f) This person broke into your house to steal from it. (**block 112**)   burglar ✓

(g) This person saw the whole thing. (**block 91**)   witness ✓

(h) This person lives next door. (**block 111**)   neighbour ✓

(i) This person plays 'up front' in a game. (**block 96**)   forward ✓

(j) This person tries to solve crimes. (**block 102**)   detective ✓

(k) This person is next to the 'head' or principal. (**block 104**)   deputy ✓

Exercise 3 — The **coloured** word in each sentence is **misspelt**. Write the correct form.

(a) Mary brought home a lovely little statue as a suevenir of her holiday to Greece.

souvenir / ~~suvenior~~.

(b) The point at which a river joins the sea is called an estueary. _____

(c) A regular amount of physicle exercise is an important element of a healthy lifestyle.

physical /

(d) 'I don't mean to embarass you, but you've got some egg on your chin.'

embarass /

(e) It is said that curiousity killed the cat.

curiousouity /

(f) Stamp and coin collecting can be enjoyable hobbys.

hobbies /

(g) It is the responsability of the driver to ensure that all passengers wear a seatbelt.

responsability /

(h) She asked for permision to stay up late to see the end of the movie.

permission /

(i) Good grammer is necessary for good writing.

grammar /

(j) A person who listens is a lissener.

listener /

(k) Febury is the second month of the year.

February /

(l) Autum is called the 'Fall' in America.

Autumn /

Exercise 4 — **Alphabetical Order**

List all the words that end with **-y** from **blocks 101** to **112** in column **A**.
Then sort them alphabetically in column **B**.

a b c d e f g h i j k l m n o p q r s t u v w x y z

A list

1. democracy
2. deputy
3. precisely
4. practically
5. responsability
6. Laboratory
7. cruelty
8. estuary
9. curiosity
10. secretary
11. valley
12. jewellery
13. cruelly

AlphaBetical list

1. c r u e l l y /
2. c r u e l t y /
3. c u r i o s i t y /
4. d e m o c r a c y /
5. d e p u t y /
6. e s t u a r y /
7. j e w e l l e r y /
8. l a b o r a t o r y /
9. p r a c t i c a l l y /
10. p r e c i s e l y /
11. r e s p o n s i b i l i t y /
12. s e c r e t a r y /
13. v a l l e y /

Exercise 1 It is often difficult to know whether words end in **-ic** or **-ck**.
In general, words of one syllable end in **-ick**, e.g. click, sick.
Words of two or more syllables usually end in **-ic**, e.g. terrific.
Locate the words that illustrate this rule from the numbered **blocks**.

(a) attic ✓ (bl 8)   (b) organic ✓ (bl 25)

(c) ~~traffic~~ sympathetic (bl 34)   (d) democratic ✓ (bl 101)

(e) tragic ✓ (bl 81)   (f) terrific ✓ (bl 38)

(g) miggick ✓ (bl 80)   (h) scientist ✓ (bl 85)

(i) prehistoric ✓ (bl 68)   (j) magic ✓ (bl 81)

(k) basic ✓ (bl 81)   (l) traffic ✓ (bl 35)

and one to break the rule miggick. ✓ (bl 80)

Exercise 2 **Crack the code!**
Find **block** words by solving these codes.
All words are between **blocks 1** and **28**.

a	e	i	o	u		s	n	f	l	t	r	p	y
2	3	4	5	–		*	9	7	8	1	6	;	=

(a) | * | 2 | 7 | 3 | 1 | = |

s a f e t y ✓

(b) | 4 | 9 | 1 | 3 | 9 | * | 3 |

i n t e n s e ✓

(c) | 2 | * | 1 | 6 | 2 | = |

a s t r a y ✓

(d) | 8 | 4 | * | 1 | 3 | 9 | 3 | 6 |

l i s t e n e r

(e) | ; | 5 | * | 4 | 1 | 4 | 5 | 9 |

p o s i t i o n ✓

(f) | 4 | 9 | 1 | 3 | 6 | 3 | * | 1 |

i n t e r e s t

(g) | 2 | ; | ; | 8 | 2 | – | * | 3 |

a p p l a u s e ✓

(h) | 5 | ; | 3 | 6 | 2 | 1 | 3 |

o p e r a t e ✓

(i) | * | 3 | ; | 2 | 6 | 2 | 1 | 3 |

s e p a r a t e ✓

(j) | 4 | 9 | 1 | 3 | 6 | 9 | 2 | 8 |

i n t e r n e l ✓

Exercise 3 — Antonyms

Write **block** words with opposite meanings to each of the following.

(a) failure   _success_   (bl 36)   (b) unattractive   _attractive_   (bl 8)

(c) masculine   _feminine_   (bl 29)   (d) compulsory   _necessary_   (bl 21)

(e) permanent   _temporary_   (bl 21)   (f) negative   _positive_   (bl 12)

(g) sweet   _bitter_   (bl 10)   (h) detach   _attach_   (bl 8)

(i) basement   _attic_   (bl 8)   (j) native   _foreigner_   (bl 56)

(k) rude   _polite_   (bl 11)   (l) acceptance   _refusal_   (bl 47)

Exercise 4

The **coloured** word in each sentence is **misspelt**. Write the correct form.

(a) The performance will commense at eight. (Wk 12)   _commence_

(b) We took the elivator to reach the top floor. (Wk 13)   _elevator_

(c) The annual carnivel in Rio de Janeiro is spectacular. (Wk 14)   _carnival_

(d) An oath in court is a solumn promise to tell the truth. (Wk 15)   _solemn_

(e) 'Let's forget it. It's not worth having an arguement over.' (Wk 2)   _argument_

(f) The factory was closed as a precaution after the hazardous chemacle spillage. (Wk 3)   _chemical_

(g) The Incas were an ancient civilizasion from Peru. (Wk 4)   _civilisation_

(h) The class prepared well for the examanation. (Wk 5)   _examination_

Exercise 5

Complete these analogies using **block** words.

(a) instinct is to instinctive as distinct is to...   _distinctive_

(b) male is to female as masculine is to...   _feminine_

(c) drink is to thirsty as eat is to...   _hungry_

(d) musician is to orchestra as singer is to...   _show_ _choir_

(e) rectangle is to rectangular as circle is to...   _circular_

(f) outside is to external as inside is to...   _internal_

(g) magic is to magician as politics is to...   _politician_

(h) out is to exit as in is to...   _enter_

(i) metre is to height as kilogramme is to...   _weight_

(j) eastern is to western as southern is to...   _northern_

(k) minus is to negative as plus is to...   _positive_

(l) lose is to win as failure is to...   _success_

week 34 General Revision

Exercise 1 Let's remind ourselves of the most common way of making the **l** sound at the end of words. We use **-le** most of the time – but there are some occasions when **-el** is the right choice. Choose **-le** or **-el** to make these words complete.

le or el

(a) coup + *le* = *couple* ✓
(b) obstac + *le* = *obstacle* ✓
(c) hurd + *le* = *hurdle* ✓
(d) scribb + *le* = *scribble* ✓
(e) tunn + *el* = *tunnel* ✓
(f) chis + *el* = *chisel* ✓
(g) gigg + *le* = *giggle* ✓
(h) syllab + *le* = *syllable* ✓
(i) jew + *el* = *jewel* ✓
(j) responsib + *le* = *responsible* ✓
(k) purp + *le* = *purple* ✓
(l) profitab + *le* = *profitable* ✓

Exercise 2 Write the correct form of the **misspelt** word in each sentence. The misspelt words are **coloured**.

(a) It is most important to have a high standard of hygeine in food preparation areas. — *hygiene* ✓

(b) During the trial a mystereous figure lurked at the back of the courtroom. — *mysterious* ✓

(c) The populeation of the country is set to rise for a number of years to come. — *population* ✓

(d) It won't be long now before we are in secondery school. — *secondary* ✓

(e) She was knocked unconscience in the fall from the horse. — *unconscious* ✓

(f) Unfortunately, there was a long delay in getting an apointment to see the doctor. — *appointment* ✓

(g) She called the jeweler to check if her chain was fixed. — *jeweller* ✓

(h) The next comittee meeting was set for the last Friday in January. — *committee* ✓

(i) It is hard to know what kind of occupeation you will end up with as an adult. — *occupation* ✓

(j) We listened to the wedder forecast last night. — *weather* ✓

(k) I ate a biskit for my supper. — *biscuit* ✓

(l) My brother's son is my little neview. — *nephew* ✓

(m) August, September and October are the months of autum. — *Autumn* ✓

Exercise 3

Locate the **block** words from the list in this **wordsearch**.
The words are written in a **V**-shape.

a	c	u	t	o	r	a	e	e	x	a	l	d	i	m
o	p	h	r	i	c	o	s	q	t	a	n	a	d	o
c	u	o	o	l	v	i	v	t	u	u	n	e	y	t
c	h	a	l	e	g	o	v	n	o	t	s	r	e	s
o	h	i	s	o	v	c	l	i	w	i	a	e	y	s
p	r	o	v	d	i	o	i	u	l	t	s	e	i	o
i	n	g	a	n	e	e	h	l	n	l	t	o	d	y
a	n	l	a	i	s	s	u	t	a	y	e	s	p	
a	r	t	a	n	m	a	p	r	r	r	i	y	h	e
e	r	r	e	i	n	t	g	e	a	r	n	t	r	e
o	x	u	t	x	c	i	m	t	x	o	a	c	m	t
c	k	t	e	n	c	n	n	r	i	t	e	e	p	l
h	i	a	i	h	e	e	s	t	a	a	r	u	l	e
m	u	t	c	z	t	o	p	n	e	w	r	h	u	i
t	i	n	i	u	n	g	s	a	l	r	m	g	o	n

1. apologise ✓
2. voluntary ✓
3. exception ✓
4. desperate ✓
5. civilised ✓
6. intense ✓
7. hurried ✓
8. interrupt ✓
9. astound ✓
10. extreme ✓
11. citizen
12. organic ✓
13. extinct ✓
14. chose ✓
15. hunch ✓
16. equal ✓
17. choir ✓
18. chill ✓
19. acute ✓
20. argue ✓

Exercise 4

The word **sci / ent / ist** can be broken into **three** syllables.
Sort these words into groups of **two-**, **three-** or **four-**syllable words.

hunter	military	recommend	mathematics	intend
recognise	marmalade	expert	courageous	civil
scientific	reflection	caterpillar	tennis	majority

two syllables

hun/ter ✓
ex/pert ✓
ten/nis ✓
in/tend ✓
ci/vil ✓

three syllables

re/cog/nise ✓
mar/ma/lade ✓
re/flec/tion ✓
re/com/mend ✓
cour/age/ous ✓

four syllables

sci/en/ti/fic ✓
mi/li/ta/ry ✓
ca/ter/pi/llar ✓
ma/the/ma/tics ✓
ma/jo/ri/ty ✓

Exercise 1 — Dictionary Work
Write the **block** words that match these dictionary definitions.

(a) to break in on an activity (**wk 1**) — *interfere*

(b) a person engaged in politics (**wk 3**) — *politician*

(c) the enclosing boundary of a circle (**wk 4**) — *circumference*

(d) highly priced or costly (**wk 5**) — *expensive*

(e) one of a series of connected scenes (**wk 9**) — *episode*

(f) something that stops progress (**wk 11**) — *objection*

(g) the first or highest in rank (**wk 14**) — *principal*

Exercise 2
Locate the **block** words from the list in this **wordsearch**.
The words are written in a **V**-shape.

o	o	c	c	e	n	f	a	n	b	d	e	n	d	y
l	l	c	o	a	n	p	l	y	i	u	m	l	i	r
s	e	n	e	o	t	n	r	u	g	r	i	m	o	i
n	t	g	u	s	o	a	s	o	l	i	t	s	a	r
y	o	a	e	i	d	b	l	e	f	s	s	e	m	a
g	t	i	t	n	c	b	n	j	o	e	h	r	n	s
o	n	y	p	c	o	o	u	h	p	u	e	e	l	e
a	u	r	p	d	o	i	y	i	y	d	u	s	n	d
c	u	s	s	h	q	l	p	p	l	g	r	e	i	a
f	u	p	u	d	l	n	l	y	a	a	i	u	m	b
f	o	u	r	a	g	l	r	e	a	m	n	c	e	s
f	o	r	e	i	g	a	t	n	e	r	i	e	u	c
o	l	r	e	l	m	a	p	e	s	t	v	n	e	a
g	u	e	t	c	n	o	g	p	n	o	n	v	s	c
l	a	i	c	u	e	p	s	e	r	s	l	u	o	i

1. legendary
2. professor
3. catalogue
4. fluid
5. colleague
6. hygiene
7. foreign
8. primary
9. usually
10. approve
11. station
12. builder
13. typhoon
14. solve
15. build
16. minus
17. fortunate
18. ocean
19. druid
20. agent

Spelling Record Card

	Week 1	✓ ✗	Week 2	✓ ✗	Week 3	✓ ✗	Week 4	✓ ✗	Week 5	✓ ✗
1										
2										
3										
4										
5										
6										
7										
8										
9										
10										
11										
12										
13										
14										
15										
16										
17										
18										
19										
20										
21										
22										
23										
24										
25										
	Score: /25		Score: /25		Score: /25		Score: /25		Score: /25	

Teacher's Signature:_____   Parent/Guardian's Signature: _____

Spelling Record Card

	Week 6	✓ ✗	Week 7	✓ ✗	Week 8	✓ ✗	Week 10	✓ ✗	Week 11	✓ ✗
1										
2										
3										
4										
5										
6										
7										
8										
9										
10										
11										
12										
13										
14										
15										
16										
17										
18										
19										
20										
21										
22										
23										
24										
25										
	Score: /25		Score: /25		Score: /25		Score: /25		Score: /25	

Teacher's Signature:_____   Parent/Guardian's Signature: _____

Spelling Record Card

	Week 12	✓ ✗	Week 13	✓ ✗	Week 14	✓ ✗	Week 15	✓ ✗	Week 17	✓ ✗
1										
2										
3										
4										
5										
6										
7										
8										
9										
10										
11										
12										
13										
14										
15										
16										
17										
18										
19										
20										
21										
22										
23										
24										
25										
	Score: /25		Score: /25		Score: /25		Score: /25		Score: /25	

Teacher's Signature:_____   Parent/Guardian's Signature: _____

Spelling Record Card

	Week 18	✓ ✗	Week 19	✓ ✗	Week 20	✓ ✗	Week 21	✓ ✗	Week 22	✓ ✗
1										
2										
3										
4										
5										
6										
7										
8										
9										
10										
11										
12										
13										
14										
15										
16										
17										
18										
19										
20										
21										
22										
23										
24										
25										
	Score: /25		Score: /25		Score: /25		Score: /25		Score: /25	

Teacher's Signature:_____   Parent/Guardian's Signature: _____

Spelling Record Card

	Week 23	✓✗	Week 25	✓✗	Week 26	✓✗	Week 27	✓✗	Week 28	✓✗
1										
2										
3										
4										
5										
6										
7										
8										
9										
10										
11										
12										
13										
14										
15										
16										
17										
18										
19										
20										
21										
22										
23										
24										
25										
	Score: /25		Score: /25		Score: /25		Score: /25		Score: /25	

Teacher's Signature:_____   Parent/Guardian's Signature: _____

Spelling Record Card

	Week 29	✓/✗	Week 30	✓/✗	Week 31	✓/✗				
1										
2										
3										
4										
5										
6										
7										
8										
9										
10										
11										
12										
13										
14										
15										
16										
17										
18										
19										
20										
21										
22										
23										
24										
25										
	Score: /25		Score: /25		Score: /25					

Teacher's Signature:_____   Parent/Guardian's Signature: _____

Spelling Record Card

	Weeks 1-7	✓ ✗	Weeks 9-15	✓ ✗	Weeks 17-23	✓ ✗	Weeks 25-31	✓ ✗	
1									
2									
3									
4									
5									
6									
7									
8									
9									
10									
11									
12									
13									
14									
15									
16									
17									
18									
19									
20									
21									
22									
23									
24									
25									
	Score: /25		Score: /25		Score: /25		Score: /25		

Teacher's Signature:_____   Parent/Guardian's Signature: _____

Pupil's name:

Class:

	Week 1	Week 2	Week 3	Week 4	Week 5	Week 6	Week 7	Week 9	Week 10	Week 11	Week 12	Week 13	Week 14	Week 15	Week 17	Week 18	Week 19	Week 20	Week 21	Week 22	Week 23	Week 25	Week 26	Week 27	Week 28	Week 29	Week 30	Week 31	Wks 1-7	Wks 9-15	Wks 17-23	Wks 25-31
25																																
24																																
23																																
22																																
21																																
20																																
19																																
18																																
17																																
16																																
15																																
14																																
13																																
12																																
11																																
10																																
9																																
8																																
7																																
6																																
5																																
4																																
3																																
2																																
1																																

Colour one space for each correct spelling in each week's test. See how well you do from week to week. Set yourself a target. Aim to reach it. Then try to improve on it.